CONSOLIDATED UPDATE

to the

Register of Qualified Huguenot Ancestors

of

The National Huguenot Society

Fifth Edition

2012

NATIONAL HUGUENOT SOCIETY
—— LIBERTY FAITH ——

Compiled by

Nancy Wright Brennan, Genealogist General

and

Jeannine Kallal, President General

San Antonio, Texas
THE NATIONAL HUGUENOT SOCIETY, INC.

Published by The National Huguenot Society, Inc.

Library of Congress Control Number: 2016943223
ISBN #978-0-9883154-2-6

Compiled and Indexed by Nancy Wright Brennan and Jeannine Sheldon Kallal
Cover Design by Janice Murphy Lorenz, J.D.
Edited by Janice Murphy Lorenz, J.D.

Printed in the United States of America by Lightning Source

CONTENTS

OBJECTIVES OF THE NATIONAL HUGUENOT SOCIETY

The objectives of The National Huguenot Society are patriotic, religious, historical, and educational. Their design is to perpetuate the memory, the spirit, and the deeds of the men and women in France called Huguenots who, because of persecution there on account of the basic tenets of their faith and their devotion to liberty, emigrated either directly or through other countries to North America and contributed by their character and ability to the development of the United States.

To achieve these objectives, the National Society aims specifically –
1. To give expression to Huguenot tenets of faith and liberty, and to promote understanding thereof, for the good and welfare of the United States;
2. To coordinate the activities of Member Societies in the States, Territories, and the District of Columbia, for the promotion and fulfilment of their common aim and purposes;
3. To encourage and foster the organization of Member Societies in those States and Territories of the United States where none currently exists and in the District of Columbia; and
4. To support the aims and purposes of the Member Societies, which shall be:
   a. To perpetuate the memory and to promote the principles and virtues of the Huguenots;
   b. To commemorate the great events in their history; and
   c. To collect and preserve historical data and relics illustrative of Huguenot life, manners, and customs.

INDIVIDUAL MEMBERSHIP

Individuals may be eligible for membership in one of our 30 active state member societies as a regular member, if he:
- is of the Protestant faith,
- is age sixteen (16) years of age or older,
- adheres to the Huguenot principles of faith and liberty and
- is lineally descended in the male or female line from
   a. A Huguenot, without regard to ethnic origin or adherence to any particular sect of Protestantism, who, subsequent to 10 December 1520 and prior to the promulgation on 28 November 1787 of the Edict of Toleration, emigrated to North America or some other country; or
   b. A Huguenot who, in spite of religious persecution, remained in France. (The word "France" in this section shall mean any territory lying within the Kingdom of France on the date of the promulgation of the Edict of Toleration, 28 November 1787.); and
- is approved for membership by the state member society he is applying to join.

INTRODUCTION

We are indeed fortunate to have such talented and industrious genealogists at The National Huguenot Society as our current Genealogist General, Nancy Wright Brennan, and our current President General, Jeannine Sheldon Kallal. After authoring the Register of Approved Huguenot Ancestors of the National Huguenot Society, Fifth Edition 2012, they have continuously updated it, and are now prepared to release this Consolidated Update. All of the changes and corrections made necessary by additional information and review are published here, including the new ancestors which have been approved, revised and expanded ancestor lineages, additions, corrections, closed lines, and an index to all.

Sometime after publication of this Consolidated Update, we will incorporate this Consolidated Update into a new *Ancestor Register*, which will be offered for sale to our members and the public to assist in their Huguenot research.

It is always a joy to discover one's Huguenot heritage, and we continue to welcome new members to The National Huguenot Society.

In Huguenot Faith from the Heart,

Janice Murphy Lorenz, J.D.
Honorary President General
August 2016

BAERDAN/BERDAN, Jan

b. France

Fled to Amsterdam, HOL; then to New Amsterdam, NY with wife and son Jan/John
in the latter part of the 17th century and settled at New Amersfoort, Flatlands (Flatbush),
L.I., NY

m/1, XX

m/2, Merretie X of Bergen, Kings Co. NY; she d. in the latter part of the 17th century

CHILD, m/1:

Jan/John[2], m. 20 May 1693, Flatlands, Eva Van Siclen/Sickelen/Sycklin (b. 1666),
d/o Ferdinandus Van Siclen/Sichgelen and Eva Antonis Jansen; moved to Hackensack, a.
1708.

CHILDREN:

Marretie[3], b. 1694, Flatlands; m/1, 16 Mar 1717, Hackensack, Joris Doremus, s/o
Cornelius Doremus – at least **5 sons**; m/2, 1733, Jacob Tietsoort

Jan[3], bp. 1695; m. 11 May1738, Crystyntje Van Giesan – **4 sons, 3 daus**

Eva[3], b. 1696/7; m. 17 Sep 1720, Cornelis Kip (bp.1 Jan 1700), s/o Nicasius
Hendrickse Kip & Antie Pieterse Breyant/Breyandt, grs/o Hendrick Hendickszen
& Anna de Sille, grgrs/o Ruloff de Kype; **1 son, 8 daus**

Ferdinandus[3], bp. 28 Jan 1700, Hackensack

Albert[3], bp. 25 Jan 1702; m. 29 Sep 1727, Divertje Banta (bp. 24 May 1710), d/o Jacob
Hendricks Banta and Jannetje Van Horn, **2 sons, 4 daus**

Willemtje[3], bp. 5 Jun 1704; m. 30 Mar 1723, Isaac Kip (bp.1697), bro/o Cornelis (above);
1 son, 2 daus

Reynier[3], b. 1705; m. 3 Nov 1738, Hackensack, Antjen Romeyne, d/o Daniel
Clasen Romeyne/Romein/Romlyn & Maritie Westervelt – at least **1 son**

Elena/Helena[3], bp. 1708; m. 30 Mar 1728, Jacob Kip (bp. 16 Dec 1702), bro/o Cornelis
and Isaac (above)

Dirck[3], b. Feb 1712; m. c. 9 Jun 1738 (banns), Antje Van Winkle – **2 sons**

David[3], bp. 1714; m. 12 May 1738, Christyntje Romeyne, sis/o Antjen, above

Annetjen[3], bp. 1 Jun 1718, Hackensack; m. 10 Dec 1736, Abraham Laroe/
LeRoux/LaRue/Larew (bp.18 Mar 1705) s/o Jacques LeRoux/LaRue/ Larew &
Wybregh Hendricks – at least **1 son**

Stephen[3], unmar.

CHILDREN, m/2:

2 daughters[3] – no further info

REF: BASS, Frank N., *Bass-Jones Genealogy,* Charissa T. Bass, publisher (Freeport Il 1931);
LABAW, George Warner, *Preakness and the Preakness Reformed Church Passaic County, NJ,*
Board of Publication of the Reformed Church in America (New York, 1902); PURPLE, Edwin
R., *Contributions to the History of Ancient Families of New Amsterdam and New York*, NEHGS
(Boston, 2013) original copyright 1881; NELSON, William and SHRINER Charles A., *History
of Paterson and its Environs (The Silk City) Vol. II,* Lewis Historical Publishing Company New
York and Chicago 1920); *2012 Register of Qualified Huguenot Ancestors,* pp. 150-1, 261-2, 315-
316.

CHÂTEL/CHASTEL/CASTELL/CASTILE/CASTLE, Edmond du

b. c. 1665, prob. Flanders – his family, Chastel de Blangerval, resided in Flanders; his parents may have been Cornelius & Agnes (Moye) du Châtel/Chastel; the arms: "Azure a chevron between 3 crosslets fitchy gold" and a crest: "A castle of three towers domed and vaned, the midmost higher than the others"

c. 1682/3 – to Philadelphia; Edmund was one of the 1st French residents of Philadelphia
10 Sep 1683 – took Oath of Allegiance in Philadelphia;

m. 1 May 1693, Philadelphia, Christian Von Bon, d/o Gerbelius/Cornelius Von Bon, a Swedish immigrant, who arr in America 20 Oct 1683 on the "America"; family was in Philadelphia and Delaware Counties, PA; family became known as Bon(e)/Bonde; Christian d. a. 25 Nov 1714, wp; 27 Nov 1714, her sister Wenetie Collett (wife of Jeremiah Collett) renounced her right to be the executrix; her estate was valued at £489 2s 2d; Christian also had a bro Abraham, a wealthy merchant in Philadelphia whose family lived on Front St. at Morris Alley, nr. Penn's Landing; he was one of the wealthiest men in Philadelphia

1707 – during Queen Anne's War, he commanded the sloop "Resolution" which sailed under letters of marque to prey upon French and Spanish commerce

d. a. 2 Mar 1713/4, wp, Philadelphia, PA; left an estate worth £506 16s 2d; his will is signed "Edmond Du Castell"; all his property was left to his wife who, in turn, devised it to their children by her will

CHILDREN:

Samuel[2], in mother's will; no further info

Edmund II[2], b. c. 1695, Philadelphia; c. 1713, surveyed land in MD and patented it in 1715 when he settled on St. John's or Piscataway Creek, Prince Georges Co, MD, on an estate of 300, acres named "Casteel"; he was a tobacco planter; m. c. 1714, Johanna/Hannah (Acres?) - had at least 2 sons, Edmund III[3] who m. Rebecca X and had 10 ch and Meshach[3]; Johanna d. c. 1733 and he d. p. Nov 1743 – they left no wills; Johanna may have been his 2nd wife – some say he m/1 Mary Amos and had a dau – not proven

Christian[2], m. 17 Apr 1720, Christ Ch, Philadelphia, James Allen

REF: HOYE, Charles E., The Hoyes of Maryland (1942); Marriages Recorded by the Registrar General of the Province, 1685-1689; DUNAWAY, Wayland Fuller, "The French Racial Strain in Colonial Pennsylvania" in The Pennsylvania Magazine of History & Biography, Vol. 53, #3 (Oct 1929); FOSDICK, Lucian J., The French Blood in America (NY, 1911); NEHGS, Seventh Part of A Roll of Arms (Boston, 1958. LOUDON, Phyllis Casteel & LEHMAN, Mary Jean Johnson, History of the Casteel Family.

GOUX/GOUD, Jean George

b. 26 Feb 1703, bp. 28 Feb 1703, Étobon, Haute Saône Dépt. Franche-Comté, FR, w. of Belfort, s/o Daniel Goux & Elizabeth Flénnet

m/1, 19 Aug 1727, Étobon, Elizabeth Balet, d/o the late Nicolas Balet, master refiner at the iron works at Chagey, s.e. of Étobon; she d. 27 Feb 1732, Étobon

m/2, 13 May 1732, Étobon, Anne Duperret, d/o David Duperret, originally from Rougemont in the Canton de Berne [Switzerland]; she d. a.1 Feb 1763 when 3ʳᵈ wife Rachel was named in a deed

1751 - left FR for America in the *Priscilla*, via Germany and the Dutch port of Rotterdam, arr Boston with a group of German and French refugees; settled on the bank of the Kennebec River, in Maine

9 Apr 1760 - John George Goud of Pownalborough, farmer, granted Town Lot # 3 on the Kennebec River containing 22 acres; required to build house, clear 5 acres within 3 yrs & work on the ministerial lot 2 days a yr. for 10 yrs. Granted 100 acre Lot # 9 on east bank of the Eastern River; same rqmts as previous grant

m/3, Rachel X, named in deed 1 Feb 1763

1 Feb 1763 - John George Goud of Pownalborough, yeomen, sold Lot # 3 to Jonathan Bowman for £100; John's wife Rachel relinquished her dower right in the property

12 Jun 1772 - John George Goud of Pownalborough, yeoman, sold 100 acre Lot # 9 to James Goud of Pownalborough, yeoman, for £130

d. p. 12 Jun 1772, ME

CHILDREN, m/1:

Elizabeth[2], bp. 25 Jul 1728, Étobon, presented by Lazare Balet, refiner at the iron works at Chagey, and Elizabeth Flénnet for her daughter Elizabeth Goux. She was living at the time of her mother's death in 1732

Jean George[2], bp. privately by the minister due to the child's feebleness; later publicly bp. 22 Jan 1730, Étobon; d. & bur 24 Jan 1730, Étobon, aged 2 days

CHILDREN, m/2:

Pierre[2], bp. 15 Feb 1733, Étobon, presented by Pierre Kauffmann and by Jeanne Plançon, assisting her daughter Anne Marthe Bugnon; he d. 24 Oct, 1750, bur. Étobon, the following day, aged 17 yrs, 8 mo

Susanne[2], bp. 12 Oct 1735, Étobon; her godfather was Pierre Abraham Goux, son of Daniel Goux *le vieux* [the elder], *laboureur* [plowman] of Étobon, and her godmother was Susanne Goux, d/o Daniel Goux, *laboureur* of Étobon, who, because she was a minor, was represented by her mother, Catherine Bonhôtal; she d. 1 Aug 1748, bur. Étobon the following day, aged 13 years

Jacques/James[2], bp. 23 Sep 1738, Étobon; his godfather was Jacque Goux, son of Daniel Goux *le vieux*, *laboureur* of Étobon, and his godmother was Anne Catherine Plançon, dau/o Pierre Plançon *le jeune* [the younger] of Étobon, a minor who was represented by her mother, Elizabeth Goux. On 9 Apr 1760, James [English for Jacques] Goud of Powanalborough, farmer, granted 100 acre Lot # 16 on the e. bank of the Eastern River; On 2 Jun 1766, James Goud of Pownalborough, yeoman, sold the south half of 100 acre Lot # 16 to James Malbone of Pownalborough for £33.6s.8d. Rachel Margaret Goud, his wife, relinquished her dower rights and signed the deed with her husband who signed as "Jaque Goud"; On 4 Dec 1778, James Goud of Pownalborough, yeoman, sold the northern half of 100 acre Lot # 16 to Jonathan Reed for £120, his wife Rachel Margaret relinquished her dower rights and put her mark on the deed as Margaret Goud - her husband signed as Jacque Goud

GOUX/GOUD, Jean George (continued)

> CHILDREN: m/1 –
> **Margaret**[3], b.29 Jul 1772;
> **Rachel**[3], b. 11 Jun 1788;
> **James**[3], b. 13 Jun 1790;
> **Ezekiel**[3], b. 26 Oct 1792
> CHILDREN m/2 –
> **William**[3], b 29 Jun 1795;
> **Charlotte**[3], b. 30 Apr 1797;
> **Nancy**[3], b. 14 Feb 1799;
> **John Turner**[3], b. 8 Jan 1801;
> **Martha**[3], b. 8 Oct 1802;
> **Clarkson**[3], b. 23 Dec 1805? m/3 –Joanna X, **issue unk**

Anne Françoise[2], bp. 5 Mar 1742, Étobon; her godparents were Pierre Abraham Goux, *sabotier* [woodenshoe –*sabot*- maker] of Étobon, and his wife, Anne François Dubois; she m. Samuel Goodwin Jr (b. 16 Feb 1740)
> CHILDREN:
> **Lydia**[3], b. 5 Mar 1763, d. 22 Jan 1841, unm;
> **Ann**[3], b. 13 Jan 1765, m. 1 Jan 1798, Jonathan Bowman;
> **Samuel Twycross**[3], b. 3 Nov 1766, m. Elizabeth Holland;
> **George**[3], b. 8 Nov 1768, m. Sarah Houdelette;
> **Charles**[3], b. 12 Nov 1770

Lazare[2], bp. 24 Aug 1744, Étobon; his godfather was Lazare Ballet, master refiner at the iron works at Chagey, and his godmother was Charlotte Léopoldine Carlin. On 10 Oct 1770, Lazarus Goud of Pownalborough, yeoman, was granted a 60 acre lot in Pownalborough "lying back of the one hundred acre Lotts on the Eastern Side of the Eastern River...." Revolutionary War Service; he m. 12 Feb 1785, Winthrop, ME, Rahannas McGarry (Mignerey?); he d. 3 Aug 1819
> CHILDREN:
> **Betsey**[3], b. 28 Mar 1786;
> **Rachel**[3], b. 18 Dec 1789;
> **George**[3], b 28 Jan 1791;
> **Lurania**[3], b 27 Jan 1793

Jean George[2], bp.1 Jan 1748, at the church of Étobon; his godparents were Jean Migneré, *laboureur et charbonnier* [coalman/charcoal burner] of Étobon, and his wife Elizabeth Pourchot; he d. 8 Apr 1749, bur. the next day in the cemetery of Étobon, aged 15 months

REF: NEHGR Research Services Case M012811B & M012811B-2 citing Parish Register, Église reformé d'Étobon (Haute-Saône) France and Lincoln Co., Maine Land Records; ALLEN, Charles E, "A Huguenot Settlement in Maine in *The Nation*, Vol. LVI:141 (1893); STACKPOLE, Everett S., *History of Winthrop,* p. 403 (1944); ALLEN, Charles, *History of Dresden*, pp.175-6 (1931); Revolutionary War Pension and Bounty-Land Warrant Application Files, 1800-1900 #4,152, Goud Lazarus/Rahannas.

GUILLE/GUIL/GUYL/GIL, Isaac

prob. b. in Mézières-en-Drouais, Eure-et-Loir Dépt., Centre, s.e. of Dreux; several Guille families were there in the 16th and 17th centuries

m. 29 Nov 1665, Anne Boucelaire in the Protestant Church of Drouais in Fontaine, n.e. of Querre

went to London; Isaac, Anne/Anna and ch Magdelene, John, Peter, Stephen and Joseph are in the London Registers

by 1685/6, the family was in Henrico Co, VA; Isaac and Anne with children – they were imported by Richard Kennon who rec. land for their importation

CHILDREN (baptisms in the Protestant Church of Drouais):

Madelaine/Magdelene[2], bp. 20 Dec 1666

Jean/John[2], bp. 27 Feb 1668; naturalized in VA, 12 May 1705

Pierre/Peter[2], bp. Dec 1669; bound to Gilbert Elam, Sr. on 1 Feb 1686

Étienne/Stephen[2], bp. 20 Sep 1676; m. Martha X; bound to John Steward on 1 Feb 1686; naturalized in VA, 12 May 1705

> CHILDREN:
>
> **William**[3], bp. 20 Jan 1720/1
>
> **Amy**[3], b. 25 May, bp. 30 Aug 1729

Joseph[2], b. 1677; m. Elizabeth X; bound to Thomas Pouldon on 1 June 1686; naturalized in VA 12 May 1705; will dated 19 June 1732, probated 6 Nov 1732 names wife and children, Peter, Joseph, Jacob, Francis, William and Ann.

> CHILDREN:
>
> **Peter**[3]
>
> **Joseph**[3,] a. 1711; m c. 1735 Elizabeth Gates d/o William and Susannah (Epps) Gates
>
>> CHILDREN:
>>
>> **Jane**[4], m. John Sullins
>>
>> **Joseph**[4], b. a. 1747 in Henrico Co. VA, d. p.1810 in Oglethorpe Co. GA, m. c. 1780 Martha Hopson d/o Cpn. Henry and Martha (Neville) Hopson
>
> **Jacob**[3]
>
> **Francis**[3], b.c. 1712, will dated 21 Sep 1791 in Chesterfield Co. VA names wife, Martha sons, Francis, Philip, Stephen, Jacob, Joseph, James daughters Martha, Jenny and Milly Wells
>
> **William**[3]
>
> **Ann**[3], b. 30 May, bp. 15 Jun 1733

REF: Church recs – Fontaine; London I Registers; GHIRELL, Michael, *A List of Emigrants from England to America, 1682-1692*; Henrico Co. Record Book, #2 (1685/6); CLARK, Eva Turner, *Gill Abstracts from Records in Southern States and Genealogical Notes* (New York 1939); TONEY, Benjamin C., "Some Descendants of Isaac and Anna (Boucelaire) Guille/Gill a Huguenot Family", http://sciway3.net/clark/gill/HuguenorGill.html

HENCH, Johannes

b.c. 1711/12 Metz, France; fled to Germany

1743, to PA but returned to GER to marry, back to PA in 1749

m. a. 1 Sep 1749, Christina Schneider (1713-1789)

by 1753 in Chester Co., PA; on tax lists 1756-64, 1774, 1778 and 1787

d. a. 9 Dec 1801, wp; bur. Juniata Co. PA

CHILDREN

Peter[2]

Henry[2]

John[2] b. 15 May 1750; m. Margaret Rice, a. 1780 (c. 1762-1821) John d. 20 Nov 1800; Rev.
War service PA, 1777; bur. Loysville, Perry Co, PA; **5 sons 8 dau**

Jacob[2] m. Susanna Rice; **3 sons 3 dau**

George[2]

Maria Elizabeth[2]

Christina[2]

Elizabeth (Betsy)[2]

REF: EMIG, Lelia Dromgold, Records *of the Annual Hench and Dromgold Reunion* The United Evangelical Press, (Harrisburg, PA) 1913; FLICKINGER, Robert Elliott, *Flickinger Family,* University of Michigan, 1927; *The Jeremiah Hench Family 1743-1973.*

LAPRADE, Andrew
b. 1665, France
c. 1688, in James City County. VA
m. c. 1695, Ann X (d. 9 Feb 1726
d. 1 Feb 1726, prob. VA
CHILDREN:

John[2], b. 1702; d. a. 18 Oct 1784, wp, Goochland Co. VA; lived near Williamsburg, James City Co., VA. Had one section of land in the Manakin Colony on the east side of the James River in Goochland Co. and one on the west side, aka the south bank, of the James River
   m/1, XX
   CHILDREN, m/1:
   Andrew[3], b. 1733, Henrico Co. VA; m. Martha X; d. 16 Apr 1778, Valley Forge during the Rev. War
      CHILDREN:
      Elizabeth[4], b. 30 Mar 1759
      Mary[4], b. 9 Jul 1760; m. 13 Feb 1779, Valentine Cunningham
      John[4], b. 25 Feb 1763; m/1, 8 Dec. 1785, Phebe Elam; m/2, Sarah X; the 2 marriages produced a total of 22 ch – **17 sons, 5 daus**; he d. a. 8 Feb 1836, wp, Chesterfield Co. VA
      Nancy[4], b. 27 Jul 1765; m. Jun 1787, William Owen
      William[4], b. 27 Jan 1767; m. Mary Watkins
      Martha[4], b. 15 Jul 1770; m. Jesse Hatcher
      Hannah[4], b.30 May 1773; m. John Miles
      Andrew[4], b. 23 Mar 1777; m. Ann Kelcher
   Ann[3], m. 1 Jul 1762, Richard Pleasants
   m/2, Temperance Ferrar
   CHILD, m/2:
   Joanna[3], b. 12 Jan 1749, bp. 12 Feb 1758; m. 19 Mar 1772, William Miller
   m/3, Anna Williams
   CHILD, m/3:
   Mary[3], b. 10 Feb 1753
   m/4, 10 Aug 1760, Susannah Walley
   CHILDREN, m/4:
   Martha[3], b. 9 May 1761, bp. 12 Jul 1761; m. Gideon Hatcher
   Judith[3], b. 5 Jul 1763, bp. 1 Aug 1763; m. Anderson Peers
   John[3], b. 16 Mar 1766, bp. 23 Jul 1766
   Susannah[3], b. 14 May 1768, bp. 28 Aug 1768
   Betty[3], b. 23 Jun 1770, bp. 22 Sep 1770
Andrew[2], b. c. 1711, m. Elizabeth X, wd. 5 Oct 1765 Chesterfield Co. VA, ch **John** and **Rachel** named in will along w/gson Daniel Young. Wit. And'w Laprade, Jr. (probably son b. 1733 d. 29 Apr 1797 in Chesterfield Co. VA, m. Martha Flourney, d/o Francis Flourney & w/2 Mary Gibson, grgrgr/dau/o Laurent & Gabrielle (Mellin) Flourney/Flournoy
Elizabeth[2], m. c. 1747, Antoine LeVillain (d. a 13 Mar 1750), s/o Jean & Olympe (X) LeVillian; she m/2, 1751, X Young; m/3, 9 Aug 1753, Joseph Starkie/Starkey
   CHILD, m/1:
   Mary[3], b. 1748

LAPRADE, Andrew (continued)

REF: Virginia State Library Archives Division, LaPrade Family Bible Records, 1757-1798;] KNORR, Catherine Lindsay, *Marriage Bonds and Ministers' Returns of Chesterfield County, Virginia, 1771-1815* (1958); *The American Genealogist,* Vol.42, #1; JONES, W. Mac., editor, *The Douglas Register*, (J.W. Fergusson & Sons, Richmond Virginia, 1928); *Descendants of Andrew LaPrade,* a family document owned by Bill Miller. WOOD, Betty Rozell, *Ancestors and Descendants William Thomas Rozell and Almena Hill Madison County, Alabama,* (B.R. Wood, Huntsville AL 2004); WEISIGER, Benjamin B, III, *Chesterfield County, Virginia Wills 1749-1774.*

PECHIN, John George

   b. c. 1717, France; fled to Germany

   m. Catherine X

   1752 - settled in Maine; granted 40 acres of land in Frankfort "in the Eastern part of the Province lying within the Neck of land between Kenebeck River and the River called the Eastern River".

   1765 - in Pownalborough, Lincoln Co. MA (ME District)*.

   d. c.1774

   CHILD:

   Frederick[2], b. c. 1750/3; 1766, in Pownalboro, Lincoln Co., ME m. Mary X; he d. 15 Aug 1778, Rev. War

   CHILDREN:

   Isaac[3], bp. 7 Feb 1774, Pownalborough; m/2, 29 Jul 1804, Thankful Page (1786-1861); War of 1812 pension for Isaac names widow Thankful; he d. c. 1830; used name **Pishon/Pishen**

   CHILD:

   Isaiah[4], b. 13 Dec 1804, Penobscot, ME; m. 6 May 1827, Abigail Knowlen (1808-1889) - she m/2, Benjamin Wood; Isaiah d. 1844, Aroostook, ME; at least **1 son, 3 dau** and possibly others.

   Abigail[3], bp. 7 Feb 1774, Pownalborough

   Mary[3], bp. 7 Feb 1774, Pownalborough

   Charles[3], bp. 7 Feb 1774, Pownalborough

*Between 1667-1780, Maine was part of Massachusetts. Until Maine became a state in 1820, it was called "the district of Maine in Massachusetts". Pownalborough is now Wiscasset.

REF: ALLEN, Charles Edwin, *History of Dresden, Maine; Formerly a Part of the Old Town of Pownalborough* (1931) and *Some Huguenot and Other Early Settlers on the Kennebec* (Harvard College Library, 1892); Collections of the Maine Historical Society Vol. 8; *Magazine of New England History,* Vol. 3 & 4; BARTLETT, William S. Bartlet, A.M., Frontier Missionary: A Memoir of the Life of the Rev. Jacob Bailey, A.M., Missionary at Pownalborough, Maine (Boston, 1853); FOSDICK, Lucien John, *The French Blood in America,* (Fleming H. Revell Co., 1906); INGLE, Edward, *Christopher Pechin (1737-1779), His Ancestry and Descendants, 1706-1914 and William (1773-1849), His Ancestry and Descendants (1591-1914)* digital books at Familysearch.org/films #273484, 1394632.

PÉRON, Jehan

m. 7 Mar 1577, Salle St.-Yon, La Rochelle, Marie Pineau; he d. a. 1580
CHILD:
Jean[2], m. 22 Jun 1603, Salle St.-Michel, La Rochelle, Marie Peneau
CHILDREN, bp. Calvinist churches, La Rochelle:
Jean[3], b. 27 Mar 1604, bp. 31 Mar 1604, Grand Temple
Luc[3], b. 20 Jun 1608, bp. Salle St-Yon; m. Marie Mouchard
CHILD:
Marthe[4], b. 10 Jul 1646, bp. 15 Jul 1646, Temple de la Villeneuve; she was the
last of Luc's ch; m. 22 Jun 1670, Aytré, s.e. of La Rochelle, <u>Pierre
L'Hommedieu</u> (b. 27 Aug 1631, bp. 31 Aug 1631, Temple de la
Villeneuve-d. 24 Nov 1679, bur. 25 Nov 1679, in the Temple cemetery);
abt 1685, she left FR, *may* have gone to ENG – her sons Benjamin and
Jean were there
CHILDREN:
Benjamin[5], 27 Sep 1687, naturalized in NY
Jean/John[5], 27 Sep 1687, naturalized in NY
Osée[5], was in London, 1702
Renée[3], b. 1609-1613
Suzanne[3], b. 20 Jun 1614, bp. 29 Jun 1614, Salle St.-Yon
François[3], b.10 Nov. 1615, bp. Grand Temple

REF: Church records from La Rochelle and Québec

RUINE, Simon de

b. 1615, Hainault, France

m. 1639, Landrecies (in Nord Dépt., Nord Pas-de-Calais, s.e. of Valenciennes), Magdalena Van Der Stratten/Straeten, dau/o Lodowycke Vander Straeten fled to Amsterdam

1659 - on the ship "Faith" to New Amsterdam and settled in New Harlem

1666 - moved to Flushing

d. a. 13 Jun 1678, wp

CHILDREN

Jacomina[2] b. 1648 near Landrecies; d. 1691; m. 1668, John Demarêts (1645-1719), s/o David & Marie (Sohier) Demarêts; **3 sons, 5 daus**

Jannetie [2] b. Amsterdam m. John DePré (as his 2nd wife) 1659; John b. 1635; **2 sons, 3 daus**

Maria[2] bp. 1 Jan 1662; m. 11 Aug 1678, Samuel Demarêts (5 Aug 1656-a.19 Oct 1728, wp), s/o David & Marie (Sohier) Demarêts ; **4 sons, 6 daus**

REF: McBRIDE, Virginia, *Parratt-Perkins Progress Report 1962,* pg. 105 (Honolulu, Hawaii) 1962 RIKER, James, *Revised History of Harlem (City of New York) Its Origin and Early Annals* pg. 100, 191, 350 & more; DEMAREST, Voorhis David *The Demarest Family* Volume 1 (Hackensack, NJ) 1964

TACQUET(TE)/TACKETT, Louis/Lewis

b. c. 1670/75, FR; sister? Rachel (b. c. 1655) m. William Spiller and had a son Wm. Spiller

1686/87 - transported from England to Virginia, passage paid by Englishman Nicholas Hayward; also on the list of transportees were Louis/Lewis Reynaud/Reno, Jean de la Chaumette/Shumate and others.

1711 - he had a small land patent in Stafford Co. along with other Huguenots

m. c. 1708, Mary Sarah Spiller (1680, ENG-2 Oct 1764, VA), d/o William & Mary (X) Spiller; Spiller land distributed in the will of William[2]

1710/11 - proprietary land grant in Stafford Co. with Louis Reynaud/Reno; he had a mill in Stafford Co. on Aquia Creek – one of the earliest in that county, built to serve the Huguenot settlement

1723 - listed on Tenders of Tobacco in Overwharton Parish with Lewis Tacquet, Jr., John Tacquet, Lewis Renoe, William Spiller; Overwharton Par. is now in Pr. Wm., Loudon, Fairfax and Alexandria Co.

d. 1744, Cedar Run, Pr. Wm. Co. (which is now the area of Quantico USMC Base)

CHILDREN:

Louis/Lewis[2], b. 1709, VA, poss. Stafford Co.; m. c. 1729/0, Mary X; he d. 1764, prob. Frederick Co, VA

    CHILDREN:

    Lewis[3], b. c.1730, Stafford Co, VA; m. a. 1764, Mary/Polly Crace; d. p 1823, Kanawha Co. WV; Rev. War, patriotic service; **3 sons, 4 daus Keziah**[4] m. John Young

    George[3]?, b. c. 1732

    Thomas[3], b. c. 1734

    Francis[3], b. 1736; m. Sarah Rice; d.1798, VA (now WV); **issue**

    John[3], b. 1737; m. Joanna X – at least 1 dau Sarah; d. 1800, Monroe Co, VA **(now WV)**

        CHILD:

        Sarah[4], m. c. 1783, Greenbrier Co, WV, Elijah Cremeans, s/o Higgins & Sarah (Anders) Cremeans; she d. 13 Mar 1874, Cabell Co, WV; **issue**

    Christopher[3], b. 1740; m/1, XX; m/2, a. 1762, Hannah Dehart; he d. 27 Aug 1790, Ft. Tackett, Kanawha Co, VA (now WV)

        CHILDREN, m/1:

        Lewis[4], m. Mary Busham

        Son

    Peter[3], b. 1750; m. Lydia X; d. 1776, VA

    Elizabeth/Betsy[3], b. 1772 or 1780-85; m. Reuben Cremeans (1763, MD-2 Aug 1853, Mason Co, VA), s/o Higgins & Eleanor (Wall) Cremeans **OR** m. John McElhany (conflicting evidence: 1850 Cabell Co., VA census indicates Elizabeth age 65 and Reuben age 91 which questions that she was a daughter of Lewis who d. 1764. One source states that Elizabeth was b. c. 1766 and was the d. of Ambrose Tackett. Higgins' will proved 5 June 1837 lists wife Sarah, 6 daus and "older children" Elijah, Reuben, Sinsey, Burton, Moses, Elizabeth Clang and Milly Clagg.)

John[2], b. 1712, Cedar Run, VA; m. Rosannah X; he d. 1774, Rowan Co, NC

    CHILDREN:

    William[3], b. c. 1737; m/1, Susannah Sumpter (1770-1824, KY), d/o Edward & Claudine Ann (Buester) Sumpter; m/2, 1762, Rachel Ramey; he d. 1835, KY   not sure that there was a 2nd mar; issue m/1

    John[3], b. 1745; m. c. 1777 Barbara Kabler, dau/o Conrad Kabler; d. 1851, SC

TACQUET(TE)/TACKETT, Louis/Lewis (continued)

> Philip[3], Moses? b. c. 1745, Pr. Wm. Co, VA; m. Sarah X; d. 1 Jan 1839, Pike Co, KY; **issue**
>
> Lewis[3], b. 1748, Pr. Wm Co, VA; m. Delilah Gentry b. 1755 NC, d. p 1850; Lewis d. 1800, Spartanburg, SC; **issue**
>
> James[3], b. 1750; d. 1810, Adair Co, KY
>
> Francis[3]
>
> + 1 other

Rachel[2], b. 1714; m/1, X Spiller, m/2, Moses Jeffries; she d. 1791

William[2], b. 1722; m/1. a. 1744, Sarah Waters (b. c. 1722, VA-1766); m/2, c. 1758, Cedar Run, Stafford Co., VA, Elizabeth Stamps (b. a. 1741, VA-d. 1794), d/o Thomas & Mary (Rose) Stamps; he d. a. 8 Apr 1783, wp, prob. Dettingen Parish, Pr. Wm. Co, VA; he was a bondsman for William Spiller's will. Wm. Tackett's will (dated 30 Jun 1782) mentions wife Elizabeth, sons Lewis, William, daus Elizabeth Reno, Mary Hedges, grdau Mildred Reno

CHILDREN, m/1:

> **Elizabeth**[3] (b. c. 1744, VA), m. c. 1760, VA, Lewis Reno (1740, Pr. Wm Co, VA-Sep 1799, Muhlenberg Co, KY), s/o Lewis & Elizabeth (Whitledge) Reno and a direct descendant of <u>Louis de Reneau/Reno</u>; **issue**
>
> **Mary**[3] (b. c. 1750, VA); m/1, X Hedges/Hodges; m/2, William Butler; m/3, John Gallahue
>
> **William**[3], c. 1751; m. c. 1770, Frances/Fanny Reno (b. c. 1743, Pr. Wm Co, VA-a. 2 Oct 1797, wp, Pr. Wm Co), d/o Francis & Elizabeth (Bayliss) Reno and a direct descendant of <u>Louis de Reneau/Reno</u>; he d. c. 1810; **issue**

CHILD, m/2:

> **Lewis**[3] (b. 1753

*d/o Daniel & Rachel (Johnson) Remey, grd/o James & Elizabeth (Sanders?) Remy, grgrdau/o William & Catherine (Asbury) Remy, grgrgrdau/o <u>Jacques & Mary (X) Rémy</u>

<u>NOTE</u>: Pr. Wm Co formed, 1731, from Stafford (1664) and King William (1702); Fauquier Co. formed, 1759, from Prince William

REF: HARRISON, Fairfax, *Landmarks of Old Prince William* (Chesapeake Book Co. 1964), pp. 188-190; KING, George Harrison Sanford, compiler, *The Register of Overwharton Parish Stafford County, Virginia, 1723-1728, and Sundry Historical and Genealogical Notes,* (Fredericksburg, VA, 1961), p. 159; LANG, Mae Elizabeth, compiler, *The Tackett-Fletcher Pioneers and Supplement* (St. Joseph, IL,1973); MANAHAN, John E., Editor, *The Huguenot Publication no. 25, 1971-1973* (The Society Founders of Manakin in the Colony of Virginia, Inc.), pp. 166-167; ALBERT, Billie E. Taylor *Digging Up Bones;* Dorman, John F., *Culpepper Co. VA Deeds, Vols. 2 & 6; American Pioneers,1967-1970, Vols.4-7;* will of William[2] Tackett, 1783, in Will Book G (1778-1791), Prince William Co, VA; LANG, Mae Elizabeth, The Tackett-Fletcher Pioneers & Supplement (1973)

REVISED OR EXPANDED ANCESTOR LINEAGES

BONNEAU, Jean

> b. La Rochelle, FR
> m. Catherine Roi
> CHILD:
> **Antoine**[2], b. 27 Jan 1647, La Rochelle, FR; m. 1678, Catherine de Bloys/DuBliss; fled La Rochelle, 1685; c. 1686/90 – emigrated to the Carolinas; naturalized there; d. c. 1700, in the Carolinas
> CHILDREN :
> **Jean Henri**[3], b. La Rochelle; to SC with father
> **Ant(h)oine**[3], b. 1680, La Rochelle; m. p. 24 Sep 1702 (date of marr contract), Jeanne Elizabeth Videau, b.1685 (rec. 18 Nov 1685 London Church), d/o <u>Pierre & Jeanne Elizabeth (Mauzé) Videau</u> of Berkley Co, VA; Antoine was liv. Charleston where he was a cooper; held several civic offices; d. p. 20 Feb 1742, wd - a. 8 Feb 1743, wp, Berkley Co, VA; his will mentions **5** sons and **6** daus but does not include his wife Jeanne who must have d. a. 20 Feb 1742 when his will was dated.
> CHILDREN:
>> **Anthony**[4], b. 1710, SC; m.c. 1731/5, Margaret Henriette Horry (1713-3 Apr 1761), d/o <u>Élias & Margaret (Huger) Horry</u>
>> **Henry**[4,] m. Sarah Dutarque
>> **Peter**[4,] d. 1748, m. Esther Simons
>> **Samuel**[4], (1725-1788), <u>m/1</u>, Frances de Longuemare, <u>m/2</u>, 1759, Mary Jermain/Germain) Boisseau, (1726-1791) wid/o <u>David Boisseau</u> - 2 daus
>>> **Elizabeth**[5], m. Ezekiel Pickens, s/o Gen. Andrew & Rebecca (Calhoun) Pickens (Rebecca was the sis/o John Ewing Calhoun) – **3 sons** (no known issue), **1 dau**
>>> **Floride**[5], m. 8 Oct 1786, John Ewing Calhoun (he d. 1802) – their dau **Floride**[6] (b. 1792) m. John C. Calhoun (1782-1850), Vice President of the U.S., 1825-1832 – **issue**
>> **Benjamin**[4]
>> **Elizabeth**[4], m. Samuel Simons
>> **Catherine**[4], m. X Nicholson
>> **Mary**[4], m. Joshua Toomer, **3 sons**
>> **Floride**[4]
>> **Judith**[4]
>> **Est(h)er**[4]
> **Jacob**[3], b. Carolina, bef. 1695, m. Jane Videau, dau. of <u>Pierre and Jeanne Elizabeth Mauzé Videau</u>, **3 sons**
> **Mary**[3], m. Nicholas Bochet who d. 1733, **4 sons**

BONNEAU, Jean (continued)

REF: *Transactions of the Huguenot Society of SC,* #37 (1932) – will of Antoine Jr, #51 (1946), #79 (1974), #84 (1979); *SC Historical & Genealogical Magazine*, Vol. XXV (1924), Vol. XV (1914); *SC A Guide to the Palmetto State*; RAVANEL, Daniel, *Liste des François et Suisses* (1868, reprint 1968); *Cross of Languedoc* (Aug 1984) SALLEY, A.S., Jr., *Marriages in "The SC Gazette & its Successors, 1732-1801* (1902); SIMPSON, R.W., *History of the Old Pendleton District* (1913)

BRASSEUR/BRASHIER/BRASHEAR, Robert II

b. c. 1595/98, FR; a Benois Brasseur was chr 1595, at Bouches-du-Rhône, s/o Robert I; [Benois was Robert II's bro]; Bouches-du-Rhône is not a town, it is a dépt. in Provence on the Mediterrean; not <u>certain</u> that this is the same family as below

m. XX, prob. in FR

prob. left Fr during the 1620's; said to have emigrated, with his bros Benois/Benjamin and Thomas, to the Isle of Thanet, ENG, which is in the extreme n.e. of Co. Kent, N. Foreland area,

1 Jun 1636 - Robert renewed a promissory note in Warrisquicke/Warrosquyoake, VA (became the Isle of Wight Co. in 1637), so had prob. been in VA for a few yrs

24 Feb 1638 - he and Peter Rey were granted 600 acres in Upper Norfolk Co. on the Nansemond River, a tributary of the James

6 Oct 1640 - rec 100 acres in Upper Norfolk on the Nansemond for transportation of 2 servants

7 Oct 1640 - Thomas Pursell was mentioned as a servant to Robert Brasseur, having been transported

12 Apr 1653 – additional land was granted for a group of persons, incl. Mary, Persid. Persis, Kathe, and Bennet Brasseur – prob. his ch; more grants later to Ann, Benjamin Sr., Martha, Mary Sr., Robert Jr. & Susanna

1663 - Benjamin, Jr., Elizabeth & John emigrated to VA; Thomas went to VA in 1677

Robert d. p. 4 Dec 1665, wd – a. 16 Dec 1665, wp, Calvert Co, MD; left estate to 3 men; no ch, grch mentioned; estate to a cousin Mary; court amended it and appointed a guardian for Robert, s/o Benjamin

CHILDREN:

(There is some confusion as to whether Robert II was the f/o or bro/o Benois; the evidence at hand suggests that Robert II was his father – any additional <u>proof</u> is encouraged.)

Benois(t)/Benjamin[2], b. c. 1619/20, FR; m. Marie/Mary (Richford?), who m/2, Thomas Sterling; settled Nansemond Co, VA, by 1653, to MD, 1658, settling in Calvert Co; 4 Dec 1662, naturalized in MD as "late of VA and subject of the crown of France"; d. Dec 1662, Calvert Co, MD; Mary's will was probated, 25 May 1663, names sons Robert, Benjamin, John; daus Mary, Anne, Susanna, Martha, Elizabeth

CHILDREN (birthdates/order not certain):

Robert IV[3], b. c. 1646; <u>m/1</u>, XX (mother of at least 2, if not all, of 3 his ch), <u>m/2</u>, 1679, Mrs. Alice (Spriggs?) Jackson, widow of Thomas Jackson; he d. 1712, Prince George's Co, MD; **issue**

Benjamin[3], b. c. 1647, d. Feb 1676, unmarr – left estate to sis Martha

John[3], b. c. 1649; m. Anne (Dalrymple or Sterling?); d. 1696; prob. no issue as no ch mentioned in his will

Mary[3], b. c. 1650; <u>m/1</u>, 7 May 1669, Nathanial Robbins, <u>m/2</u>, c. 1688, Christopher Ellis; she d. p. 23 Jan 1702, when she was named the heir of William Osborne's estate; she prob. d. Prince George's Co, MD

CHILDREN:

Elizabeth[4], b. 15 Jun 1689, Queen Anne Parish, Prince George's Co, MD

Agniss[4]. 29 Aug 1697, Queen Anne Parish, Prince George's Co, MD

Christopher[4], b. 29 Jun 1698, Queen Anne Parish, Prince George's Co, MD

Ann[3], b. c. 1652; m. c. 1685, prob. William Dalrymple, Jr.

Susanna[3], b. c. 1655; m. c. 1679, prob. <u>Mareen Duvall</u>; she. d. 1692; **issue**

BRASSEUR/BRASHIER/BRASHEAR, Robert II (continued)

      Martha[3], b. c. 1658; m. 1674 Henry Kent, Jr.; **issue**

      Elizabeth[3], b.c. 1660; <u>m/1</u>, John Sellman - **issue**, <u>m/2</u>, 8 Nov 1708, Dr. William Nichols

Mary[2], b. c. 1622; d. young

John[2], b.c. 1624 FR; <u>m/1</u>, Mary Cocke; <u>m/2</u>, Mary Pitt; was his father Robert's heir & inherited land in Nansemond Co.; became a Quaker

Thomas[2], b.c. 1626

Persi(d)e[2], b. c. 1628; m. poss. John Cobreath

Robert III[2], b. c. 1630; m. Florence (Rey?); d. 5 Dec 1665; **no issue**

Katherine[2], b. c. 1632; poss. m. Mark Clare

Martha[2], b. c. 1636, Isle of Wight Co, VA, <u>m/1</u>, c. 1657, VA, Capt. William Moseley (1624-c. 1683/4); <u>m/2</u>, a. Nov 1684 ,VA, George Taylor; she d. p. 1684

      CHILDREN, m/1

      Elizabeth[3], m. c. 1689, John Hawkins, of Old Rappahannock Co, VA

      Edward[3], b. 1662; m. Elizabeth Wilson, d/o Elias Wilson, of Sittenburne Parish, Richmond Co.; **no issue**

      Robert[3], m. c. 1694, Martha Reeves, d/o James & Elizabeth (X) Reeves; he d. May 1707; **2 sons**

      Benjamin[3], m. c. 1689, Elizabeth (Thompson) Catlett, widow of William Catlett; he d. a. 10   Dec. 1709, wp, Essex, Co, VA; **2 ch**

      William[3], b. 1660; m. Hannah Hawkins, d/o Thomas Hawkins, of old Rappahannock Co, VA; Hannah d. 1695; he d. a. 10 Apr 1700,wp, Essex Co, VA; **4 ch**

      Martha[3], m. William Thompson

Margaret[2], b. Sep 1642, Nansemond Co, VA; m. c. 1658, Thomas Fleming Jordan (1634-8 Dec 1699) s/o Thomas Jordan; d. 7 Dec 1708, Chuckatuck, Nansemond, VA (now in Suffolk Co, n.e. of city of Suffolk); became Quakers

      CHILDREN:

      Thomas[3], b. 6 Mar 1660/1; m. 6 Dec 1679, Elizabeth Burgh, d/o William Burgh, of Chuckatuck; **issue**

      John[3], b. 17 Aug 1663; m. 9 Mar 1688/9, Margaret Burgh, sis/o Elizabeth (above); he d. a. 6   May 1712 wp; **issue**

      James[3], b. 23 Nov 1665

      Robert[3], b. 11 Jul 1668

      Richard[3], b. 6 Jun 1670; m. 1706, Rebecca Rattcliff

      Joseph[3], b. 8 Jul 1672

      Benjamin[3], b. 18 Jul 1674

      Mathew[3], b. 1 Jan 1676/7; m. 5 Sep 1699, Dorothy (Newby) Bufkin, widow of Levin Bufkin (she m/3, 17 May 1750, X Davis); he d. a. 13 Oct 1748, wp; **issue**

      Samuel[3], b. 15 Apr. 1679; m. 10 Dec. 1703, Henrico Co, VA, Elizabeth Fleming (bp 28 Oct 168-, d. 20 Jul 1763; m/2 Thomas Raley), d/o Charles & Susanna (Tarlton) Fleming, of New Kent Co; Samuel d. a. 11 Jun 1719 ,wp; **issue**

      Joshua[3], b. 31 Aug. 1681; m. 1771, Elizabeth Sanbourne, d/o Daniel & Sarah (X) Sanbourne, of Isle of Wight Co; he d. p. 28 Feb 1717/8, wd; **issue**

Mary[2], b. 3 Jan 1645/6, Isle of Wight, VA, d. 1713, VA; <u>m/1</u>, c. 1664, James Biddlecombe, **issue**, <u>m/2</u>, c. 1686, Samuel Peachey, **no issue**; she d. 1713

BRASSEUR/BRASHIER/BRASHEAR, Robert II (continued)

REF: BRASHEAR, Charles & McCOY, Shirley B.- *A Brashear(s) Family History*, Vol. 1, pp. 1-15; MYRICK, Victor, *Myrick Family History* (1970), pp. 18-20; NUGENT, *Cavaliers and Pioneers,* Vol 1, p. 41; *VA Land Patents,* Book 6, pp. 72, 346 ; BRASHEAR, Henry S,, *The Brashear-Brashears Family, 1449-1929*; GRAY, Allen, *Edward Pleasants Valentine Papers,* Vol. I; *Huguenot Society of VA*, Vol. XXVIII (1956); BACK, Troy L. & BRASHEAR, Leon, *The Brashear Story* (1962); Wm. & Mary College Magazine, Vol. II (1981), Vol. III (1982), *Genealogies of VA Families*; DORMAN, John F. & MEYER, Virginia M, editors, *Adventures of Purse & Person* (1987); *Register of Queen Anne's Parish, Prince George's Co., Maryland* (microfilm #14304, MD Historical Society, Baltimore); The Maryland Calendar of Wills, 1703-1713, Vol. III (Baltimore, 1907).

BRIQUE/BRICQUET/BRICKEY, Jean de /John

b. 1640, FR, possibly Reims <u>or</u> Artois in the present Pas-de-Calais

m. Alce/Alice X, b. c. 1640, FR; d. prob. Richmond Co, VA; she survived him

c. 1680 – to America, prob. to Charles Town, SC; poss. on the *Richmond*, arr 30 Apr 1680

c. 1681 – to MD, then to VA 1690-92, 6 suits by various plaintiffs were filed against him; most were dismissed (rec. Westmoreland Co.)

d. a. 29 Oct 1718, inv., Westmoreland Co, VA

CHILDREN:

Jean/John², b. 1670, FR; m. Sarah X; he d. 19 Dec 1732, Richmond Co, VA; widow Sarah m/2, Thomas Russell

> CHILDREN (some rec. N. Farnham Parish, Richmond Co, VA):

> **Dorcas**³, m. c. 1740, Daniel <u>Rémy</u>; widow by 1774, liv. Dunmore Co, VA (now Shenandoah Co.); **no known issue**

> **Mary**, b. N. Farnham Par.; m. Thomas Wilson; d. Richmond Co, VA

> **Anne**³, b. 18/19 Feb 1726, Lunenburg Parish, Richmond Co, VA; <u>m/1</u>, Thomas Wilson, <u>m/2</u>, Daniel Jackson; d. c. 1774, Richmond Co.

> **Sarah**³, b. 19 Feb 1728/9, Lunenburg Par, Richmond Co, VA; m. William Mullen

> **Betty**³, b. 19 Feb 1731/2, N. Farnham Par, Richmond Co, VA or Cople Parish, Westmoreland Co, VA; m. John Reynolds of Cople Par., Westmoreland Co, VA

Mary², b. FR; m. Lunenburg Parish, Thomas Job; she d. 31 Oct 1774, Lunenburg Parish; **no issue**

Peter², b. FR; m. c. 1715, Winifred Lucas, d/o Charles & Temperance (Smith) Lucas; c 1730, settled VA

> CHILDREN;

> **Jarad**³, b. c. 1738, Westmoreland Co, VA; <u>m/1</u>, XX – **6 ch**, <u>m/2</u>, c. 1784, Elizabeth *prob.* Buckholder (d. a. 1807) – **4 ch**, incl. **Peter**⁴ (10 Apr 1761, VA-13 Apr 1836, Botetourt Co, VA) who m. 1ˢᵗ cousin Elizabeth⁴ Brickey; Jarad d. 7 Oct 1790, Bedford Co, VA

> **Winifred**³, m. X Kirkham; **2 ch**

> **Temperance**³, b. Westmoreland Co, VA' m. X Morgan

> **Peter**³, b. c. 1747, prob. m. Ellender X – 1 son Peter⁴, who d. a. 1 Jan 1791

> **Nancy/Ann**³, b. Westmoreland Co, VA; m. X Sanford

> **William**³, <u>m/1</u>, 9 Jan 1756, Westmoreland Co, VA, Mary Nancy Smith – **2 ch**, <u>m/2</u>, Sara Elizabeth X – **6 ch**; he d. c. 1837, Williams, Norfolk, VA

> **Dorcas**³, b. Westmoreland Co, VA; m. 30 Mar 1772, James Garner, s/o Henry Garner – **1 ch**

> **John**³, b. c. 1740/1, Westmoreland Co; <u>m/1</u>, c. 1759, Mary Elizabeth Garner; <u>m/2</u>, p. 1780, Bedford Co, VA, widow Jane (X) Scott; he d. 14 May 1806, Blount Co, TN

>> CHILDREN, m/1:

>> **Jarad**⁴, b. 10 Apr 1760, m. Amy Compton - **5 ch**

>> **Elizabeth**⁴, b. c. 1764, Westmoreland Co, VA, m. 1ˢᵗ cousin Peter⁴ Brickey, the s/o Jarad³ & Elizabeth; she d. c. 1825, Botetourt Co, VA

>> **Peter**⁴, b. 10 May 1769-d. Feb 1859, m. Nancy Smith- **no issue**

>> **Winifred**⁴, b. 5 Jan 1772, m. John Smith – **no issue**

>> **Mary**⁴, b. 17 Jul 1774, m. Jonas Jenkins

>> **John**⁴, b. 20 Mar 1776, m. Jemima Caldwell – **2 sons**

>> **William**⁴, b. 18 Feb 1780, Botetourt Co, VA, m. c. 1810, prob. TN, Eleanor

BRIQUE/BRICQUET/BRICKEY, Jean de /John (continued)

Dobkins (c. 1781, Cocke Co, TN-1860, Blount Co, TN) – **issue**; he d. 14 May 1856, Blount Co, TN

CHILD, m/2:

Sarah[4], b. c. 1785; m. James Tipton; d. 1810, bur. Blount Co, TN

REF: Brickey Family Bible (1815); BRICKEY, Raymond Luther, *The Brickey Heritage;* BRICKEY, Thomas Coke (manuscript, 1981-includes pages from previous works); BRICKEY, John, *Genealogy of the Brickey Family* (1855); BRICKEY, Lydia M. & Norville W, family history transcribed from one written by John Brickey in 1855.

FERRÉE/ Fier(r)e, Daniel (Fuehre/ Führe in GER)

b. c. 1650; family *said* to be of Torchamp, Orne Dépt, Basse-Normandie, s.w. of Domfront

m. c. 1673/4, FR, Marie de la Warenbuer/Warembur (c. 1653, Rhine [prob. means Alsace], FR-Jan 1716, bur. Ferrée/Carpenter graveyard, s. of Paradise in what is now Lancaster Co, PA); there is a family memorial stone in the All Saints Episcopal Cem. in Paradise.

fled FR to Strasbourg, then to Bavaria by 12 Sep 1681 - in Steinweiler (a sm. town s. of Landau, in the *Pfalz*) - Daniel & Maria purchased some goods on that date; on 17 Nov 1681, Daniel & Maria sold 3 cottages

a. 10 Mar 1708, Daniel died Landau, Bavaria, 18 mi. n.w. of Karlsruhe, <u>or</u> Steinweiler

10 Mar 1708 - pd. for a certificate of standing and passport to emigrate to PA, via HOL & ENG; papers signed Billigheim (now Billigheim-Ingenheim, s.e. of Landau); certificate said for <u>widow</u> Maria, her son Daniel his wife + 6 single ch (2 of whom were sons of Daniel II)

by summer, 1708 – some of the family was in ENG where they stayed for a few months – Daniel & his family, his sis Catherine & her family were granted letters of denization on

25 Aug 1708, thus giving them the right to own land in America as British citizens

mid Oct 1708 – Daniel & his wife + 2 sons, Catherine, husband Isaac LeFèvre & son sailed on the *Globe*, arr 18 Dec 1708, LI, NY

6 May 1709 – Maria arr in London from Rotterdam with the rest of the family bet Dec 1709-

bet Dec 1709-Jan 1710 – several ships sailed for NY but it wasn't until 10 April 1710 that any actually sailed; Maria with sons John , Philip, daus Jane and Mary were on one of those of those ships; they had to stay on Nutten (now Governor's) Island from June until Aug when they went up to the Hudson to Esopus (now Kingston)

Sep 1712 - 2000 acres by patent were granted by Martin Kendig in Strasburg, Chester Co (now Lancaster Co.), PA; Marie then had the patent granted in Philadelphia, 12 Sep 1712, to son Daniel & son-in-law Isaac – cost was £150; Marie founded the Huguenot Colony in Pequea Valley, PA; all 6 of her ch were each given 333 acres of land, the remaining 2 acres were apparently for her

CHILDREN:

Daniel II[2], b. 1676/7; m. c. 1700, Steinweiler, Anna Maria Leininger (b. 1678); he obtained a certificate from the Reformed Walloon Ch of Pelican, Steinweiler, for him and his family attesting to the fact that the family was of the "pure Reformed religion" and were faithful members of the church, dated 10 May 1708; d. a. 9 Aug 1762, adm

CHILDREN:

Andrew[3], bp 28 Sep 1701, Steinweiler; m. Mary Reed; he d. 20 Dec 1735, Lancaster Co., PA; **4 sons, 1 dau**; dau **Lydia**[4] (1731-1778) m. c. 1751, cousin Samuel[3] LeFèvre (28 Jun 1719, PA-4 May 1789, PA), s/o <u>Isaac & Catherine (Ferrée)[2] LeFèvre</u>

John[3], b. 2 Feb, bp 8 Feb 1702/3, Rohrbach (sm. town bet Landau & Steinweiler); m. c. 1725, Lancaster Co., PA, Barbara Stautenberger; d. 1735; **4 sons, 1dau**

Daniel III[3], b. 1706; m. 1 May 1739, Lancaster Co., PA, Mary Carpenter, d/o Henry & Salome (Rufenu) Carpenter; became a Quaker; he d. a. 4 Sep 1750, wp, Lancaster Co., PA; **3 sons, 5 daus**

Elizabeth[3], b. 1710; <u>m/1</u>, c. 1728, 1st cousin Abraham LeFèvre (9 Apr 1706-20 Nov 1735, Lancaster Co.), s/o <u>Isaac & Catherine (Ferrée)[2] LeFèvre</u> – at least **2 sons**; <u>m/2</u>, c. 1736, Christian Kemp, s/o John & Anna (Fouerfauch) Kaempf – **2 sons, 3 daus**

Joseph[3], b. 1712, Lancaster Co., PA; m. c. 1729, Sarah Delaplaine, d/o James & Elizabeth (Shoemaker) Delaplaine; he d. p. 1789; **1 son**

FERRÉE/ Fier(r)e, Daniel (Fuehre/ Führe in GER) (continued)

Isaac[3], b. c. 1715; m/1, Elisabeth[3] Ferrée, his 1st cousin, d/o Philip[2] & Leah (DuBois) Ferrée 4 sons, 2 daus; m/2, Susan Green – 2 sons, 5 daus; Susan m/2, Joel Ferrée[3] (below); Isaac d. 2 Feb 1782, Lancaster Co., PA

Catherine[2], b. 26 Mar 1679; m. c. 1704, Bavaria, Isaac LeFèvre (26 Mar 1669, FR-1 Oct 1751, PA), s/o Abraham & XX(Antoinette Jerian?) LeFèvre; son **Abraham**[3], m. cousin Elizabeth Ferrée[3], d/o Daniel II[2] & Anna Marie (Leininger) Ferrée, son **Samuel**[3], m. cousin Lydia[4] Ferrée, d/o Andrew[3] & Mary (Reed) Ferrée; 4 sons, 2 daus

Jane[2], b. c. 1682?; m. 22 Aug 1715, New Castle, DE, Richard Davis; she d. a. 26 Oct 1754, wp, Belmont, PA; **no known issue**

Marie/Mary[2], b. c. 1683, prob. Steinweiler; m. 30 Jun 1715, New Castle, DE, Thomas Faulkner (d. Buck Co, PA, a. 8 May 1752, wp, Philadelphia); she d. a. 7 May 1745; she is referred to in some docs as Mary Katrina/Catherina/Catherine; **1 son, 5 daus**
CHILDREN (* - named in father's will):
***Jesse**[3], m. 1744, Old Swede's Ch, Wilmington, DE, Martha Smith
Catherine[3], m . 8 Nov 1736, Old Swede's Ch, Wilmington, DE, William Green – 2 of her ch in Thomas' will - Eve and Mary
***Mary**[3], m. Stephen Heard
***Eve**[3], m. Thomas Griffith
***Susanna**[3], m. 20 Dec 1737, Old Swedes Ch, Wilmington, DE, Thomas Wilson
? (female)[3], m. ? McCoy – son James in Thomas' will

Philip[2], b. 1686/7, Steinweiler; m. 2 Jun 1713, 1st Dutch Ch, Kingston, NY, Leah DuBois (16 Aug 1687, bp. 10 Oct 1687-12 Sep 1758, PA), d/o Abraham & Margaret (Deyo) DuBois (s/o Louis & Catherine (Blanchan) DuBois, d/o Chrétien Deyo); he d. 19 May 1753, Lancaster Co., PA
CHILDREN:
Abraham[3], b. Aug, 1715; m. 1738, Elizabeth Elting/Eltinge (30 Aug 1717, Esopus-7 Mar 1775, PA); **2 sons, 4 daus**
Magdalena[3], b. c. 1713; m. 24 Nov 1749, Lancaster, PA, William Buffington; she d. c. 1778, VA; **5 sons, 2 daus**
Elisabeth[3], b. 1718; m/1, 1738, her 1st cousin, Isaac Ferrée[3]; s/o Daniel[2] & Anna Maria (Leininger) Ferrée; she d. 27 May 1752, Lancaster Co., PA; **4 sons**, incl. **Jacob**[4] who m. Rachel Ferrée[4], d/o Joel[3] & Mary (Copeland) Ferrée + **2 daus**; m/2, X Ellemaker
Isaac[3], b. 1725; m. Elizabeth Forbush; he d. 1759 Rowan Co, NC, poss. scalped by Indians; **1 son, 3 daus**; surname **FREE**
Jacob[3], b. 1728; m. Barbara? Susannah? Carpenter (1738-1775), d/o Emmanuel & Catherine (Lein) Carpenter; Jacob d. 5 May 1782, Gettysburg, PA; **4 sons, 4 daus**
Philip[3], b. 24 Mar 1729/30, bp 1 Apr. 1711; m. Ann Copeland (18 Mar 1735-1807); he d. 24 1807); he d. 24 Apr. 1796, Lancaster, PA; **6 sons, 4 daus**
Joel[3], b. 19 May 1730, Lancaster Co, PA; m/1, Mary Copeland; m/2, 5 Nov 1759, Jane Johnston; m/3, Susan (Green) Ferrée, widow of Isaac[3] Ferrée (above); m/4, Sallie (X) Davis, widow; he d. 19 Jun 1801, Pittsburgh, PA; **issue** only from m/1 – dau **Rachel**[4] (1753-1782) m. Jacob Ferrée[4], s/o Isaac[3] & Elisabeth[3] (Ferrée) Ferrée
Leah[3], m. Peter Baker (b. 1710, GER); **5ch**

FERRÉE/ Fier(r)e, Daniel (Fuehre/ Führe in GER) (continued)

John[2], b. c. 1694; <u>m/1</u>, a. 1720, Mary Musgrave, d/o John & Mary (Hastings) Musgrave – **4 sons, 5 daus**; <u>m/2</u>, 4mo 10d 1736, Darby, Chester Co., PA, Ruth Buffington, d/o Thomas & Ruth (Cope) Buffington – **1 son**, **2 daus**; became a Quaker; he d. a. 8Apr 1773, Lancaster, PA

REF: DELONG, Irwin Hoch, "Inscriptions on the Tombstones in Carpenter's Graveyard, Lancaster Co, PA" in the *National Genealogical Society Quarterly*, Vol 14, #3 (Sep 1925); *Proceedings of the Huguenot Society of PA,* Vol. XXV, (1954), pp. 159-60, "Madame Marie Ferrée (Marie Warembur)"*;* HEIDGERD, William, *The American Descendants of Chrétien DuBois of Wicres, FR,* Part 2 (New Paltz, NY, 1969); ROWLEY, Homer King & Ruth McCammons, *Rowley-King & Allied Families* (Sun City, AZ, 1980) – contains transcript of   Philip's will; Will abstract from Lancaster Co, PA; "Madame Mary Ferrée & the Huguenots of Lancaster Co." – paper read before the Lancaster Co Historical Society (1917); Records from the Immanuel Episcopal Ch,   New Castle, DE; Steinweiler records from the Archives in Speyer, GER; ch ecs – Old Swedes Church; Thomas   Faulkner's will

LANDON/LANGDON, Jacques Morin de

Family said to have been a noble Norman family (1200-1500); Loudon in the Vienne Dépt., Poitou-Charentes, 39 km. s.w. of Tours may have been the origin of the family– it was a French Protestant stronghold; or poss. from s. of Nemours, Seine-et-Marne Dépt. Île-de-France, where there is a Château Landon c. 15 km. s. of Nemours; the Morin family was originally from Maine, FR, but one branch was in Normandy; the name Morin was dropped when the family went to ENG

a. FR, s/o Jacques, grs/o Jean
m. c. 1550, FR, X le Duc c.1560, went to ENG d. ENG
CHILDREN:

Jacques[2]

Nathaniel[2]

George(s)[2], b. c. 1590, ENG, prob Devonshire

m/1, c. 1610, ENG, XX; went to America c. 1640, settled in Wethersfield, CT; 1646, moved to Springfield, MA; m/2, 29 Jun 1648, Springfield, Hannah (Lambe?) Haynes, wid/o Edmund Haynes of Springfield; moved to Northampton in 1658, where he was one of the early settlers; he d. 29 Dec 1676, Northampton

CHILDREN, m/1, chr Georgeham, Devon, ENG, a town n.w. of Barnstaple, nr. the Bristol Channel:

*Anne[3], chr 11 Aug 1611

*George[3], chr 1 Jan 1613

Jean/John[3], chr 27 Jan 1618; m/1, c. 1638, Herefordshire, Hannah X, m/2, 20 Dec 1665, Farmington, CT, Mary (Seymour) Gridley (b. c. 1614), prob. d/o Robert & Elizabeth (Waller) Seymour, wid/o Thomas Gridley (d. a. 12 Jun 1655, inv); John d. 22 Jul 1689, Farmington; 12-15 ch

CHILDREN, m/1:

James[4], b.c.1638 Herfords, called "James the Elder", m Elizabeth X, arr Boston c. 1670; d. 12 Oct 1692; he had 5 liv ch at his death.

Daniel[5], b. c. 1655, Herefordshire; land grant 1676 at Bristol, MA; m. c.1681 Anne Lobdell (c.1664-a. 1698), d/o Isaac & Martha (Ward) Lobdell – 2 sons, 5 daus; went 1st to Farmington; he was a soldier in King Philip's War & rec. a soldier's grant in Bristol, RI where he was in 1689; he d. and his ch were "farmed out" to various relatives

Joseph[5], b. c. 1658, Herefordshire; to Boston, 1675; m. 1688, Bristol, to a "cousin"; he was a carpenter; d.c. 1689 no issue

Nathan[5], b. c. 1664, Herefordshire; to Boston, 1675; m. c. 1691, Hannah Bishop (1671-26 Jan 1701/2), poss. d/o Stephen & Tabitha (Wilkinson) Bishop – 3 sons, 2 daus; he was a leather worker and bricklayer in Southold; he d. 9 Mar 1718, Southold, LI, NY

Nathaniel[4], b.c. 1640, Herefordshire, no further info

David[4], b. 1650, Herefordshire, m Martha X, arr Boston c. 1670; d. 21 Jan 1725; 7 ch

Samuel[4], bp. 13 Feb 1653; m. 1676, Northampton, MA, Elizabeth (Copley) Turner, wid/o Praisever Turner; he d. 11 Aug 1683, Northampton; 2 or 3 sons

LANDON/LANGDON, Jacques Morin de (continued)

CHILDREN m/2

John[4], b. c. 1658; m. c. 1680, Northampton, Mary Salmon; he d. 1683, Farmington

Joseph[4], bp. 18 Mar 1659, Farmington; m/1, Oct 1683, Farmington, Susannah Root (d. 5 Dec 1712, Farmington), d/o John & Mary (Kilborne) Root – 5 sons, 4 daus, m/2, 19 Oct 1714, Farmington, Mary (Porter) Royce (22 Feb 1677-11 Mar 1759), d/o Thomas & Sarah (Hart) Porter, wid/o Joseph Royce; he d. 31 Mar 1736, Farmington.

Elizabeth[4], b. c.1663, Farmington; m. c. 1691, Luke Hayes/Haynes

***Joane**[3], chr 16 Sep 1625

***Margaret**[3], chr 19 Oct 1628

Deliverance[3], b. c. 1630; m/1, c. 1648, Suffield, MA, Deacon Thomas Hanchett (1621-1686), s/o John & Elizabeth (Perry) Hanchett, as his 2nd wife – 2 sons, 2 daus, m/2, 14 Dec 1686, Springfield, MA, Jonathan Burt; she d.10 Jun 1718, Suffield

Hannah[3], b. c. 1633; m. 4 Feb 1652, Springfield, Nathaniel Pritchett/Pritchard; she d. 1690, apparently no issue

unnamed dau[3], b. c. 1637, m. c. 1655, William Corbee/Corby/Corbin, servant of James Olmstead and founder of Haddam, CT; 3 sons, 2 daus; she is listed only by surname in the Founders List and in the probate of William's estate

*presumed to be ch of the same George Landon from whom Jean/John, Deliverance, Hannah, and the unnamed dau descend; christening records from Georgeham simply state that they are ch of George Landon with no other info on them.

CHILD, m/2:

Ester/Hester[3], b. 22 Aug 1649, Springfield; m. 20 Apr 1675, John Hannum, s/o William Hannum

REF: LANDON, James O., The Landon Genealogy (NY, 1928); JACOBSON, Judy, Southold Connections, Historical & Biographical Sketches of Northeastern Long Island(Baltimore, 1997); VR- Boston, Farmington, Northampton, Southold, Springfield, Suffield; MIRES, Maynard, H., "Landon; A Huguenot Tale" in The Colonial Genealogist, Vol. VII, #4 (1975).

MAROT, Jean

    b. prob. 5 Jul 1676, Viterne, Meurthe-et-Moselle, Lorraine, FR, s/o Jacques & Anne (X) Marot 1 Oct 1700 - arr at Manakintown on the 2nd convoy, the *Peter and Anthony*; he is listed as "Jean Morroe" with no mention of a wife or ch

    m. c. 1701, prob. VA, Ann X – said to have been Ann Pasteur, d/o Jean, but that has not been *proven* + the dates don't work! So, she was *not* the d/o the 1699 immigrant Jean Pasteur; she m/2, Timothy Sullivan; she d. a. Nov 1742, wp

    1704 – he was in the employ of William Byrd of Westover, Charles City Co, prob. as his secretary

    1705 – he was in Williamsburg

    24 May 1707 – he purchased land from William Robertson on which to build a tavern and applied for the license to operate it; after his death, his son-in-law James Shields (1700-1750) operated the tavern until his death in 1750 - it was then known as Shields Tavern; the original tavern disappeared a. the Civil War; in 1954, the Colonial Williamsburg Assoc. reconstructed it on the original site and it is currently in operation on E. Duke St. and is called Shields Tavern

    a. 16 Dec 1717, wp York, Co, VA; he d. as a result of an attack by one Francis Sharpe

CHILDREN:

Edith[2], m.1717, Samuel Cobb(s) (1698-1757) of Amelia Co. VA, s/o William & Mary (X) Cobbs; Samuel ran an ordinary in Williamsburg; he d. a. 28 Jul 1757, wp, Amelia Co; she d. a.2 Jul 1761, wp; **2 sons, 6 daus**

Anne[2], m/1, James Inglis (d. a. 1737) – 2 daus who d. young, m/2, James Shields (1700-1750), s/o Mingo & 2nd wife Anne (Bray) Shields – **1 son**, **2 daus***, m/3, 11 Jun 751. Henry Wetherburn, keeper of the Raleigh Tavern in Williamsburg, who d. a. 15 Dec 1760, wp – **no issue;** *one dau **Anne**[3] (b. 31 Jul 1742) m. Robert Booth Armistead – their dau Mary Marot Armistead[4] m. John Tyler III who were the parents of President John Tyler (1790-1862)

Rachel[2], m. Richard Booker, s/o Edward & Mary (Goode) Booker of Amelia Co., VA; Richard was a colonel in the Amelia Co. Militia; he d. 1750; perhaps **5 sons, 1 dau** - accounts vary!

REF: MACKENZIE, George Norbury, *Colonial Families of the United States of America*, Vol. II (Baltimore); BROCK, Robert A., *Documents Relating to the Huguenot Emigration to VA* (Baltimore,1962); *Genealogies of VA Families, from Tyler's Quarterly Historical & Genealogical Magazine*, Vol. I (Baltimore, 1981), Vol. II (Baltimore, 1982); *William & Mary College Quarterly Historical Magazine*, Vol. V (NY, 1966); Wills – York Co., VA & Amelia Co., VA.

PÉRON/PERRON dit Suire, Daniel

b. 25 Nov. 1638, prob. La Rochelle, FR; bp. 26 Dec. 1638, Château de Dompierre et Bourgneuf en Aunis, natural s/o François Péron & Jeanne Suire, Protestants from La Rochelle; Jeanne evidently later m. a Jacques Laurens and she d. p. 1 Mar 1656, wd; Bourgneuf is n. of Rochefort, now Charente-Maritime Dépt, Poitou-Charentes

18 Apr 1657 - from La Rochelle in *Le Taureau*, sent to New France by his father to represent his business interests; arr. Québec, 22 Jun 1657; settled Québec

6 Dec 1663 - Québec City, abjuration of the Protestant faith by Daniel – it was next to impossible to do business or anything else in Québec unless you were Catholic, so the "conversion" may have been a matter of convenience; although he abjured, he never signed another document showing a relationship with the Catholic Church; he was bap in a Protestant ch, his mother was Protestant and remained so until her death; he was disowned by his father after this

m. 26 Feb 1664, Château-Richer, Québec, Louise Gargotin (1637/8, Thairé, FR-7 Feb/20 May 1704, L'Ange Gardien, Québec), d/o Jacques & Françoise (Bernard) Gargotin; Thairé is a few kms s. of Bourgneuf; she m/2, 7 Jan 1679, L'Ange-Gardien, Charles-Louis Alain; Château-Richer & L'Ange- Gardien are n.e. of Québec on the St. Lawrence River name was Péron but the Catholic Society of New France added a second "r" to Péron; apparently he was a rather contentious man, appearing before the judicial courts many times; enjoyed fighting with words more than tilling the ground; he enjoyed speechifying, debating, protesting, nothing met with his approval

d. p. 11 Feb 1678/9, wd, L'Ange-Gardien, Québec

CHILDREN:

Antoine[2], b. 29 Nov. 1664, L'Ange-Gardien, Québec, bp. Château-Richer as Antoine Suire; m. 15 Jan 1691, Jeanne Tremble (1672, Château-Richer, Québec-23 Jun 1711, Québec City); he d. 26 May 1711, Québec City; Antoine was bap. with the surname **SUIRE**, his paternal grandmother's maiden name

François[2], b. 22 Feb 1666, L'Ange-Gardien, Québec, bp. as François Suire

Marie[2], bet. 1667-68?

Marie-Magdeleine[2], 5 Apr. 1670, bp. as Marie-Magdeleine Perron in L'Ange-Gardien

Jean[2], b. 10 Aug. 1673, bp. as Jean Lesuire in L'Ange-Gardien

Anne[2], b. 19 Mar 1676, bp. as (Anne) Perron in L'Ange-Gardien

REF: Institute Francophone de Généalogie et d'Historie, La Rochelle, *François Péron*; will of Jeanne Suire, wife of Jacques Laurens, in which she states that she is of the "Reformed religion" & that Daniel is her son; baptismal record of Daniel; baptismal records, L'Ange-Gardien.

RÉMY/REMEY/RAMEY, Jacques/Jacob

    b. c. 1630, Picardie, poss. Ivors, Oise Dépt, s.e. Compiègne, s/o Pierre Rémy of Ivoy, Ardennes Dépt. - not found, there is an Ivoy-le-Pré, Cher Dépt., Centre, s.e. Gien

    1650/51 - his father d. & Jacques escaped to ENG; some of his bros went to Alsace, then a part of GER – some of the German branch went to PA much later

    m/1, FR, Françoise Haldat d/o Antoine II & Madelaine (Marchand) Haldat; Antoine was the Seigneur de Bonnet; 1st went to England; no <u>known</u> children

    1654 - to VA as an indentured servant to Nicholas Spencer, Sec. of the Colony of VA; his wife travelled on another ship as she was bound to John Drayton but apparently did not survive the trip

    1661- he was a chain bearer when he surveyed land for Spencer

    21 Jul 1671 - acquired 200 acres of land in Nominee (*sic*) Forest in Cople Parish, Westmoreland Co, VA – the forest was adjacent to to the Nomini River (now Nomini Creek)

    m/2, 1671, Mary X, d/o Marmaduke & Jane (X) Miles <u>or</u> the d/o Nicholas Spencer

    29 Sep 1680 – naturalized, Westmoreland Co, VA; he d. a. 5 Dec 1721, wp; will names wife Mary, sons William & Jacob

CHILDREN, m/2:

William^2, b. 1672; m. c. 1693, Catherine Asbury, d/o Henry & Mary (X) Asbury; he d.a. 30 May 1738, wp, Westmoreland Co which mentions son **William**^{3}, heirs of **Jacob**^{3} Ramey, **Asbury**^{3}, daus **Mary**^{3} Sanders & **Catherine**^{3} Wormeth; sons **John**^{3}, **James**^{3} and **Daniel**^{3} - he was heir to his father's estate when his mother died.

CHILDREN:

William II^3, b. c. 1696, Westmoreland Co, VA; m. Barbara Byram; liv. Stafford Co, VA; d. 1758, Frederick Co, VA – **6 sons** – 2 of whom, John and James, did not marry

Jacob^3, b. c. 1698, Westmoreland Co, VA; m. Ann Carr, d/o William & Sarah (X) Carr; c. 1735/6, he d. Westmoreland Co., VA – **3 sons**, **1 dau**

Asbury^3, b. c. 1700/02; m. Hannah Elizabeth Neale, d/o Daniel & Ursula (Pressley) Neale;1759, liv. Westmoreland Co, VA - **3 sons**, **1 dau**

Mary^3, m. 19 Jun 1709, William Sanders – 1 dau **Elizabeth**^{4}

Catherine^3, m. X Wormeth

John^3, b. c. 1712; m. 6 Apr 1740, Mary Linton, grd/o William Linton; he d. 1791, Henry Co, VA – **6 sons**, **2 daus**

James^3, b. c. 1715; m. Elizabeth X; went to Frederick Co., VA; he d. 1757-60; his widow m/2, 1762/3, Thomas Cooper

Daniel^3, b. c. 1720; m. c. 1750, Dorcas <u>Brickey</u>, d/o <u>James & Sarah (X)</u> Brickey; he d. a. 1763; **no known issue**

Jacob^2, b. c. 1675, Westmoreland Co; m. c. 1699/00, Ann Sanford, d/o Robert & Ann (X) Sanford; he d. p. 23 Feb 1726, wd, Westmoreland Co. – names wife Ann, sons **John**^{3}, b. c. 1700, m/1, X Smith – **4 sons, 1 dau**, m/2, Mary (X) Sanford, wid/o Robert; **Sanford**^{3}, b. c. 1702-05, m/1, Sarah X, m/2, Ann Carter, d/o Robert Carter II, at least 1 dau **Mary** who m. c. 1750 John Connely and had issue; **Benjamin**^{3}, b. c. 1705, had **3 sons**, m/1, Ann X, m/2, X Phillips; **Jacob II**^{3}, b. c. 1710, m/ Sarah X, d. 1786/7, Loudon Co, VA; **William**^{3}, in bro Sanford's will (1787) as an invalid; **Joseph**^{3}, named the youngest son in his fa's will; **Mary**^{3}, b. c. 1715, m. c. 1730, X Carter/Cordell,

RÉMY/REMEY/RAMEY, Jacques/Jacob (continued)

she d. p. 1787; Jacob's widow Ann, m/2, a. 1735, Richard Omohundro II, she d. a. 13 Sep 1763, wp, Loudon Co, VA

REF: RHAMY, Bonnelle William, *The Remy Family in America, 1650-1942* (Ft. Wayne, IN, 1942); CROZIER, William Armstrong, *VA County Record Publications*, Vol. I, Westmoreland Co. (Hasbrouck Hgts, NJ, 1913); various wills; HAMLIN, Charles Hughes, "The Reamey Family" in *The Huguenot*, Publication #21 (1964-66); Richmond Co. Deed Book, Will Book, KING, George H.S., Richmond Co. VA Marriages, 1668-1853 (1964) – cited in HEADLEY, Robert K., Jr., *Married Well and Often, Marriages of the Northern Neck of Virginia, 1649-1800* (2003).

ROUTTES/ROOTE(S)/ROOT, Thomas

there is a town called Routes n. of Yvetot, Seine-Maritime Dépt, Haute-Normandie; surname believed to have been Norman

b. c. 1555, Badby, Northamptonshire, ENG, prob. the s/o FR immigrants

m/1, c. 1575, Badby, Ann Burrell (1559-1578)

m/2, c. 1579, Frances Russell

[1598 - there is a John Rootes & his wife Mary listed as "aliens in London", liv. Nettmakers Alley Vol. 10, Part 3, publication of The Huguenot Society of London]

prob. was the Thomas Roote who d. 5 Apr 1609, Badby

CHILD, m/1:

John I[2], b. 24 Jun 1576, Badby, Northants, ENG; m. 23 Jul 1600, Badby, Mary/Ann Russell (b. 18 Apr 1574, Badby); not clear if he emigrated or not – records in Badby of this family end in 1609; where they went is unknown; would have been in his 60's when his sons emigrated – inscription on John II's gravestone has his parents' names but there is no evidence that they are bur there as well – John II prob. wanted their names known; family oral history says that John I d. when his ch were young & that, at least John II, went to live w/ an uncle (his father's bro) who wanted John to join the army but as John had an aversion to war, he decided to emigrate

CHILDREN:

Marie[3], b. 21 Dec 1600, Badby

Susannah[3], b. 18 Oct 1603, Badby

Thomas[3], b. 16 Jan 1604/5, Badby; to America, c. 1637, went to Hartford, CT; m. XX; 1654, moved to Northampton, MA; he d. 17 Jul 1694, Northampton

    CHILDREN:

    Joseph[4] b. 1640, m. 30 Dec 1660 Hannah Haynes, who d. 28 Jan 1690/1

    Thomas[4] b. 1644, m. 3 Jul 1666 Abigail Alvord

    John[4] b. 1646, m. Mehitable, wid/o Samuel Hinsdale

    Jonathan[4], m. 22 Mar 1680 Ann Hull or Gull

    Hezekiah[4], m 12 Jul 1682 Mehitable Frary; he d. 29 Sep 1690

    Jacob[4], m. 2 Feb 1680 Mary Frary (1662-1744) He. d. 9 Aug 1731

    Sarah[4], m. 20 Mar 1679 Samuel Kellogg

John II[3], bp. 26 Feb 1608/9, Badby; to America, c. 1640; m. c. 1640, Farmington, Hartford, CT, Mary Kilborne (12 May 1619, Woodditton, Cambridgeshire, ENG-1697, Farmington, CT), d/o Thomas & Frances (Moody) Kilborne ; he d. 16 Aug 1684, Farmington, CT, & is bur. in the N. Cemetery, Somers, Tolland, CT – his tombstone reads "Descendants of the Huguenot Routtes who fled from France to England"; he left an estate valued at £819

    CHILDREN:

    John III[4], b. c. 1642, Farmington; m. 18 Oct 1664, Springfield, MA, Mary Ashley (6 Feb 1644/5, Springfield-9 Mar 1702/3, Westfield, MA), d/o Robert & Mary (X) Ashley; he d. 24 Sep 1687, Westfield, MA; **3 sons, 5 daus**

    Samuel[4], b. c. 1644, Farmington; m. Mary Orton (b. 16 May 1650, Windsor, CT), d/o Thomas & Margaret (Pell) Orton; he d. 27 Nov 1711, Westfield, MA; **no issue**

    Thomas[4], b. a. 1648 Farmington; m/1, 1670, Mary Gridley d. 1673 – **2 ch**, m/2, 7 Oct 1675, Mary Spencer (d.4 Nov 1690 Westfield) – **4 sons, 3 daus.**, m/3, 25 Jan 1692, Sarah (Dumbleton) Leonard, d/o John Dumbleton,

ROUTTES/ROOTE(S)/ROOT, Thomas (continued)

> wid/o Josiah Leonard, – **2 twin daus;** perhaps m. again p. 1694, when Sarah d., but no info
>
> **Mary**[4], b. c. 1650. Farmington; m. a. 1669, Isaac Bronson; **9 ch**
>
> **Stephen**[4], b. c. 1652, Farmington; m. Sarah Wadsworth; he d. 6 Jan 1717/8; **5 ch**
>
> **Susannah**[4], b. c. 1654. Farmington; m. 1 Oct 1683, Farmington, Joseph Langdon, s/o <u>Jean/John Langdon</u>; she d. 5 Dec 1712, Farmington; **9 ch**
>
> **Joseph**[4], b. c. 1656, Farmington; <u>m/1</u>, 17 Sep 1691, Elizabeth Warner – **1 son**, <u>m/2</u>, 3 May 1727, Ruth (Porter) Smith, d/o Thomas Porter, wid/o Samuel Smith – **1 dau**
>
> **Caleb**[4], b. c. 1658, Farmington; <u>m/1</u>, 9 Aug 1693, Westfield, MA Elizabeth Salmon, d/o Thomas Salmon – **5 ch**, <u>m/2</u>, a. 1712, X Gillette; he d. 10 Jun 1712, Farmington

REF: Cemetery Records, Somers, CT; ROOT, James Pierce, *Root Genealogical Records 1600-1870* (NYC, 1870); Vital records – Farmington, CT, Westfield, MA; Massachusetts Vital Records to 1850.

SICARD/SICORD/SEACORD, Ambroise

b. 1631, FR

m. Jeanne X (d. a. the 1698 NY census)

p. 1685- fled Mornac-sur-Seudre, Charente Maritime Dépt, Poitou-Charentes, s.e. Marennes; to ENG w/his wife, 6 ch; he was in the salt trade, a *saunier* – Marennes is located on the salt marshes

a. 1688 - to NY; 1692, to New Rochelle, NY where he bought 95 acres

1695 - letters of denization to him & 3 sons

1698 – on census; Ambroise, Daniel & wife Catherine, Jeanne

28 Mar 1701, wd - mentions ch Ambroise, Daniel, Jacques, Marie & her husband Guillaume Landrin, Silvie & her husband François Coquillet; Daniel's wife Anne one of the signers (Ambroise had his ch sign his will as proof of their approbation.)

d. p. 9 May 1710 – real estate transaction

CHILDREN:

Jacques[2], b. FR; d. young

Ambroise II[2], b. 1666, FR; m/1, a. 4 Nov. 1688, Jeanne Perron – **3 sons, 4 daus**, m/2, Jennie Sarcot?; he d. 1733, New Rochelle

Daniel[2], b. 1672, FR; m. Catherine Voertman/Woertman (b. c. 1677); he d. 1742/3; **6 sons, 3 daus**, incl daus:

Catherine[3] who m. Daniel Giraud, s/o Daniel & Jeanne (X) Giraud/Gerow,

Marie[3] (b. 1712), m. Daniel Chadayne, s/o Jean & Judith (Tilliou) Chad(e)ayne; **Isaac**[3] (1715- 1759), m. Catherine LeConte (c. 1725-a. 1771), d/o Josias II & Esther (Bertine) LeConte

Jacques/James[2], b. 1675, FR; m. 10 Apr. 1700, FR Ch., NYC, Anne Terrier; he d. p. 1743; **5 sons, 4 daus**

CHILDREN (4 of 9):

Jacques/James[3] (1699, New Rochelle-8 Nov. 1773, New Rochelle) who m. Jeanne/Jane Bonnet (9 Apr. 1703, New Rochelle-p. 1757, New Rochelle), d/o Daniel & Jeanne (Couturier) Bonnet – **9 sons, 3 daus**, incl:

James[4] (25 Jul 1729-a. 1771) m. 1st cousin Catherine Bertine (14 Oct 1735- a. 1790), d/o Pierre & Catherine (Sicard) Bertine – **1 son, 3 daus**

Catherine[4] (b. 18 Dec 1733) m. Benjamin Giraud/Gerow (b. 1739); **Mary**[4] (7 May 1742-1788) m. John Renaud (1743-1837) – **2 daus**

Israel[4] (1748-1819) m. Jane Coutant (26 Mar 1746-1 Sep 1794), d/o Jacques & Jeanne (Renaud) Coutant – **issue**

Ester[3], b. 1706, New Rochelle; m. Louis Angevine (b. 1702), grs/o Louis & Marguerite (Chalons) Angevine; she d. 1792, Scarsdale, NY; **3 sons, 5 daus**

Catherine[3], b. 1707; m. Pierre/Peter Bertine, s/o Pierre & Anne (Barron) Bertine **3 sons, 6 daus**

Jean/John[3], b. 8 Jun 1712; m. Maria Giraud/Gerow (b. c. 1727/8), sis/o Benjamin (b. 1739) above (prob.)

Jeanne[2], b. c. 1675/6; not in father's will

Marie[2], b. 1677 FR; m. Guillaume/William Landrin(e) (1666-p. 1732); **1 son, 2 daus**

Silvie[2], b. FR; m. François Coquillet; dau **Silvie**[3] m. Abraham Mabie, grgrgrs/o Pierre Mabille - **5 ch**

SICARD/SICORD/SEACORD, Ambroise (continued)

REF: GRAY, Henry David, "Early History of the Sicard-Secor Family" in the *NYGBR*, Vol. LXVIII, #4 (Oct, 1937); SEACORD, Morgan H., *Biographical Sketches & Index of the Huguenot Settlers of New Rochelle 1687-1776* (New Rochelle, 1941); FORBES, Jeanne A., *Records of the Town of New Rochelle 1699-1828* (New Rochelle, 1916) ; FROST, Josephine C., *Ancestors of Evelyn Wood Keeler, Wife of Willard Underhill Taylor* (1939); record from Charente-Maritime Archives

TRABUE, Antoine

Antoine[4], b. 21 Sep, bp. 28 Sep 1669, Cathedral of St. Jacques; **the immigrant to America**; by 15 Sep 1687, he was in Lausanne, SWI, when a document was created that said he had always professed the Reformed religion as had his parents; he was in Zurich, 29 Jul 1687, Schaffhausen, SWI, 30 Jul 1687, and finally, in the Hague, Apr 1688. Evidently he then went to ENG where he m/1, 6 Nov 1692, St. Marylebone Church, London, Catherine Gouton (d. c. 1701/3, VA); emigrated to VA, 1700; m/2, c. 1704, VA, Madeleine Verreuil (bp. 28 Jan 1685, FR Church, The Hague- d. 1731), d/o Moyse & Madeleine (Prudon/Prudomme) Verreuil; naturalized, 12 May 1705; 18 Mar 1717, he secured a tract of 522 acres in Henrico Co, "on "the gr[eat] fork of Swift Creek" claimed by him for the importation of 11 persons, all named, including "Anthony Tribue and Kath. Trebue" – evidently no issue from that marr. as no claim was made for their transportation. Antoine d. 29 Jan 1723/4, Manakintown – May 1724, wp. His widow m/2, c.1725/6, Pierre Chastain, as his 3rd wife; name in America became **STRABO(O)**.

CHILDREN (all b. Henrico, Co, VA): *as previously listed* – all are CHILDREN, m/2

ADD to the Ref: *TAG,* Vol. 83,#3 (Jan-Apr 2009), "Antoine Trabuc/Trabue (c. 1667/8-1724) of Montauban, Guyenne and Henrico County, Virginia, and His Two Wives, Further Identified" by Cameron Allen, pp. 199-203; *Registers of St. Mary Le Bone, Middlesex, 1668-1754, and of Oxford College, Vere Street, St. Mary Le Bone,1736-1754*

The above replaces the Antoine[4] entry in the 2012 book; info on children is correct.

VALLIANT, John

b. c. 1670, FR?, s/o (Jean?) & Mary (X) Valliant; mother's maiden name *poss.* Devallock, but more likely she remar & that was the name of her husband in 1685; lived in the Elephant & Castle, Picadilly (*sic*), London according to the document below (Elephant & Castle & Piccadilly are on opposite sides of the Thames – Elephant & Castle is in Southwark, it was considered "the Piccadilly of South London")

16 Oct 1685- document recorded in London says that John, w/ the consent of his mother, Mary Devallock, bound himself as an apprentice to Samuel Phillips of Lymas*, Co. Middlesex; Phillips was a mariner and John was to serve in MD for 4 years; document also mentions an uncle X Valliant of Lincoln's Inn Fields, servant to John De la Fontain, Esq. *prob. means Limehouse, a London parish, 3 mi. e. of St. Paul's

m/1, a. 1702, Mary (Frith?) who d. p. 16 Nov 1702, when she & John witnessed a land transaction [some say there was another marr between Mary & Judith to Mary (O'Malley) Dawson – <u>not proven</u>]

m/2, a. 18 Mar 1713, widow Judith X when she & John witnessed a land transaction - **no issue**; Judith m. a 3rd time after John's death; Judith was perhaps the widow of Thomas Bennett

d. p. 13 Jan 1721, wd - a. 28 May 1722, wp, Treadhaven Creek, Talbot Co, MD; mentions wife Judith, ch Mary, wife/o John Weymouth, Dorothy, wife/o Caleb Esgate, John, James, Joseph, Susanah; Treadhaven Creek is prob. in the area of Easton – today there are a couple places called Tred Avon there

CHILDREN, m/1:

John[2] b. 1696/7 m. Judith Bennett, (his step sister) dau of Thomas Bennett and Julia, John's step- mother;

   CHILDREN

   Nicholas[3] b. 1716 m. Judith X

   Thomas[3] b. 1719 d. 1796 m. Rachel Grace, had son **Thomas**[4] b. 1741 d. 1806 m. Esther X and son **John**[4] b. 1738 d. 1800/1 m. Mary LeCompte dau of Anthony LeCompte d. 1782 (son of Moses and grandson of Anthony). Anthony's will dated 19 Mar 1782 proved 9 Sep 1782 left his land to John Valiant.

   John[3] m. Elizabeth Caulk or Cook

   James[3] m. c. 15 Feb 1747/8 Talbot Co. Sarah Fairbank(s)

   Mary[3] m. John Harris

   Bennett[3]

   William[3]

James[2], d. p. 25 Oct 1732, wd - a. 8 Nov 1732, wp, Talbot Co, MD; was a carpenter; apparently had **no direct descendants**; his will mentions sisters Elizabeth Spry, Mary Wainoth, Dorothy Esgate, Susaney Clift, bros John, Joseph

Joseph[2]

Elizabeth[2], m. Thomas Spry (d. p. 13 Jan 1741, wd - a. 18 Apr 1746, wp, Talbot Co, MD); will mentions wife Elizabeth, sons Thomas, Christopher, dau Elizabeth

   CHILDREN

   Thomas[3]

   Elizabeth[3], m. Josiah Massey (1757-1789, Kent Co, MD), s/o Peter & Notley (Wright) Massey; at least **2 sons**

VALLIANT, John (continued)

> **Christopher**[3], m. Mary X; a planter; d. p. 8 Feb 1766, wd - a. 16 Jun 1767, wp, Talbot Co, MD; will mentions wife Mary, sons Thomas, Christopher, John, Francis (in that order – Christopher & Francis not of age), daus Elizabeth, Sarah, Mary, Rebecca, Eve, Lucrecia
>
> CHILDREN:
>
> **Thomas**[4],
>
> **John**[4]
>
> **Elizabeth**[4], m. Josiah Massey (b. 1757 d. p. 16 Dec 1789, wd, Kent Co, MD; will mentions wife Elizabeth, son **James Maynard**[5] & an unborn ch);
>
> **Sarah**[4];
>
> **Mary**[4]
>
> **Rebecca**[4];
>
> **Eve**[4];
>
> **Christopher**[4];
>
> **Francis**[4];
>
> **Lucrecia**[4]

Mary[2], m. John Weymouth/Wainoth

Dorothy[2], m. Caleb Esgate (d. a. 26 May 1732, wp, Talbot Co, MD – wife not in will, must have d. a. 3 May 1732 when the will was written); **issue**

Susanah[2], m. X Clift

REF: BRUMLEY, J.R. Sr. *The Valliants of Tidewater Maryland* 1990; JONES, Elias *Revised History of Dorchester County Maryland*, "History and Genealogy of the LeCompte Family" p. 396-413", The Read Taylor Press, Baltimore: 1925; LEONARD, R.B. *Talbot County Maryland Land Records*, Book 4, p. 7, Book 5, p. 4 and *Tavern in the Town*, (1992) p. 149 & 244; *The Maryland Calendar of Wills, 1720-1726*, Vol. V (1968), p. 103, *1726-1732*, Vol. VI (1968), p. 242 , 1744-1749, Vol. 9, p. 70, 1764-1767, Vol. 13, p. 186; *Lord Mayor's (London) Waiting Books*, Vol. 14, p. 432, 16 Oct 1685; MASSEY, Frank A., *Massey Genealogy Addendum* (Ft. Worth, TX); PEDEN, Henry C. Jr. & PEDEN Veronica Clarke *Talbot County Maryland Marriage References 1662-1800*, Colonial Roots (2010); PEDEN, Henry C. Jr. & WRIGHT, Edward *Colonia Families of the Eastern Shore of Maryland, Volume 13*, p. 233-239 Delmarva Roots; SEYMORE, Helen E. *Talbot County, Maryland Wills Libre JP -3 1777-1795* p. 28, March 1999.

CORRECTIONS

To *The Register of Qualified Huguenot Ancestors of The National Huguenot Society 5th Edition 2012*

p. 14 : Allée - b. c. 1640, add surname d'Ailly

p. 30: Joseph[3], etc. should be placed directly under CHILD

p. 36: Basse - Safrron - should be Saffron

p. 39: b. Caen, Normandie, etc. should be lined up with m. c. 14 Jul 1703

p. 40: indent *there are 2 other, etc.

p. 43: Bedlo - line 9 - 1800, (add comma)

p. 55: underline Jean & Catherine (X) Michaud

p. 61: BROCK, R.A., - add comma (in references)

p. 68: Bonneau – see revision

p. 88: Brasseur – see revision

p. 94: Brique/Brickey – see revision

p. 121: Coligny - in the NOTE - prob. name should be Annietta in both places

p. 124: Coquillet - remove underline from Pierre Mabille

p. 142: underline Simon and Magdalena de Ruine

p. 159: Du Four, son Andiaen – he was in his father's will, strike word "not"

p. 177: DuTrieux - Children, m/1 - Philippe - should be Philippe[2], not Philippe[2]

p. 209: Gaillard/Gaylord, Nic(h)olas II - William[3], s/o John[2], is doubtful and should not be used until further research can prove the lineage.

p. 219 and 228: Gaury/Guerre/Goree/Gory, Jean/John and Goury/Gory/Gaury/Garry, Jean appears to be a duplicated entry

p. 232: Guerin/Guerrant, Daniel - Magdeleine Trabue, add will dated 15 May 1787, proven, 16 Aug 1787; Pierre/Peter[2,] add will dated 3 Dec 1749.

p. 238 - Guion, Louis II – Anna/Susannah[2] may have m. 1701, John Lounsbury, s/o Richard & Elizabeth (Pennoyer) Lounsbury, not proven.

p. 270: la Fontaine - spacing in second line

p 276 : Lamar/Lamore/Lemar - James[4] m. Valinda Osborn, Linn, Salisbury, NC

p. 276: James[4], m. Valinda Osborn – delete no issue and add:
> CHILDREN;
> James[5], Thomas[5], Nathan[5], Ruth[5] m. Matthew Skean, dau[5] X m. Samuel Low, dau[5] X m. X Jenkins, Keziah[5] m. Alexander Smith, Osborn[5] m. Rachel Beasley
> REF: *The Grey Family and Allied Lines* by Jo White

p. 277: LaMare – indent line under Thomas[3]

p. 301: LeComte, Michel - DeGraft/DeGroff surnames not included in index

p. 326: (Le Villian) son Antoine[2], m. c. 1747, Elizabeth LaPrade, d/o Andrew & Ann (X) LaPrade

p. 326: L'Hommedieu, Benjamin - Marthe (Péron) L'Hommedieu was the d/o Luc & Marie Mouchard Péron (see Jehan Péron new ancestor entry)

p. 333: Mabille – LINE CLOSED; however, some descendants mar. into Huguenot so those lines are still eligible through the spouses – see below

p. 352: Mildred m. Col. Augustine Warner, not Washington

p. 387: Péron has an accent mark, Perron does not; add accent to Peron in last line

p. 394: Andrew II[4], and Rebecca had 3 sons (no known issue), 1 dau; add to References- SIMPSON, R.W., *History of the Old Pendleton District* (1913)

CORRECTIONS (continued)

p. 412: add REYNAUD as a possible variation of the surname; also Anne, wife of Lewis[2], *may* have been Anne de la Croix

p. 416: Hannah/Annatie - m. 31 Jan 1719, Philipsburg, Jeremias (comma after Philipsburg, then a space)

p. 422: Daniel Robert - Pierre I, comma aft SWI

p. 428: Routes/Roote(s), Root entry re-done

p. 438: Sellaire - Jean Henri/John Henry, b. 1684, FR; m. a. 1710/1, Anna Maria Briegal (c. 1690, prob. HOL-4 Nov 1765, Berks Co, PA)

p. 440: in entry 28 Mar 1701, it is Jacques' wife Anne, <u>not</u> Daniel's, who signed the will; Jacques[2], the 1st one, d. FR; the 6 lines below Jacques/James[4] should be indented; line under Isaac[4], should be indented; line below Jacque/James[2], should be indented

p. 450: 4th line of the NOTE – Dist. <u>of</u> Brandenburg

p. 464: Jan/John[3] Van Metre – his 2nd wife Margaret Mollenhauer (1687-p. 13 Aug 1745, Somerset Co, MJ)

p. 538: (Index) L'Orange, Jean Velas – add 329

CLOSED LINE

MABILLE DE NEVI/MABIE, PIERRE

p. 333 Given the problems with this entry and its predominately Dutch lines, proving a French connection is not apparent at this time. Advise that the line be closed as far as The National Huguenot Society is concerned. Previously, the lineage depended on a connection to the Mabille Family which does not seem to be the case.

INDEX

A NAME MAY APPEAR MORE THAN ONCE ON A PAGE.

C

Hannum, William, 25
Harris, John, 35
Hatcher, Jesse, 7
Hatcher,Gideon, 7
Hawkins, Hannah, 17
Hawkins, John, 17
Hawkins, Thomas, 17
Hayes/Haynes, Luke, 25
Haynes, Edmund, 24
Haynes, Hannah, 30
Haynes, Hannah (Lambe?), 24
Hayward, Nicholas, 12
Hedges/Hodges, X, 13
Hench, Christina, 6
Hench, Elizabeth (Betsy), 6
Hench, George, 6
Hench, Henry, 6
Hench, Jacob, 6
HENCH, Johannes, 6
Hench, John, 6
Hench, Maria Elizabeth, 6
Hench, Peter, 6
Hendickszen, Hendrick, 1
Hendricks, Wybregh, 1
Hinsdale, Mehitable, 30
Hinsdale, Samuel, 30
Holland, Elizabeth, 4
Hopson, Henry Cpn., 5
Hopson, Martha, 5
Hopson, Martha (Neville), 5
Horry, Elias, 14
Horry, Margaret (Huger), 14
Horry, Margaret Henriette, 14
Houdelette, Sarah, 4
Hull or Gull, Ann, 30

I

Inglis, James, 26

J

Jackson, Alice (Spriggs) Mrs., 16
Jackson, Daniel, 19
Jackson, Thomas, 16
Jeffries, Moses, 13
Jenkins, X, 37
Jerian, Antoinette, 22
Job, Thomas, 19
Johnston, Jane, 22
Jordan, Benjamin, 17
Jordan, James, 17

Jordan, John, 17
Jordan, Joseph, 17
Jordan, Joshua, 17
Jordan, Mathew, 17
Jordan, Richard, 17
Jordan, Robert, 17
Jordan, Samuel, 17
Jordan, Thomas, 17
Jordan, Thomas Jordan, 17

K

Kabler, Barbara, 12
Kabler, Conrad, 12
Kaempf, Anna (Fouerfauch), 21
Kaempf, John, 21
Kauffmann, Pierre, 3
Kelcher, Ann, 7
Kellogg, Samuel, 30
Kemp, Christian, 21
Kendig, Martin, 21
Kennon, Richard, 5
Kent, Henry Jr., 17
Kilborne, Frances (Moody), 30
Kilborne, Mary, 30
Kilborne, Thomas, 30
Kip, Cornelis, 1
Kip, Isaac, 1
Kip, Jacob, 1
Kip, Nicasius Hendrickse, 1
Knowlen, Abigail, 9
Kype, Ruloff de, 1

L

L'Hommedieu, Benjamin, 37
L'Hommedieu, Marthe (Peron), 37
L'Hommedieu, Pierre, 10
la Chaumette/Shumate, Jean, 12
la Croix, Anne de, 38
la Fontain, John De, 35
la Warenbuer/Warembur, Marie de, 21
Lamar/Lamore/Lemar, James, 37
Lamar/Lamore/Lemar, Keziah, 37
Lamar/Lamore/Lemar, Nathan, 37
Lamar/Lamore/Lemar, Osborn, 37
Lamar/Lamore/Lemar, Ruth, 37
Lamar/Lamore/Lemar, Thomas, 37
Lamar/Lamore/Lemar, X, 37
Landon/ Langdon, George(s), 24
Landon/Langdon, Anne, 24
Landon/Langdon, Daniel, 24

M

Spiller, William, 12, 13
Spiller, Wm., 12
Spiller, X, 13
Spry, Christopher, 36
Spry, Elizabeth, 35, 36
Spry, Eve, 36
Spry, Francis, 36
Spry, James Maynard, 36
Spry, John, 36
Spry, Lucrecia, 36
Spry, Mary, 36
Spry, Rebecca, 36
Spry, Sarah, 36
Spry, Thomas, 35, 36
Stamps, Elizabeth, 13
Stamps, Mary (Rose), 13
Stamps, Thomas, 13
Starkie/Starkey, Joseph, 7
Stautenberger, Barbara, 21
Sterling, Anne, 16
Sterling, Thomas, 16
Steward, John, 5
STRABO(O), 34
SUIRE, Antoine, 27
Suire, Daniel, 27
Suire, Jeanne, 27
Sullins, John, 5
Sullivan, Timothy, 26
Sumpter, Ann (Buester), 12
Sumpter, Edward, 12
Sumpter, Susannah, 12

T

Tackett, Ambrose, 12
Tacquet(te)/ Tackett, Keziah, 12
Tacquet(te)/ Tackett, Lewis, 12
Tacquet(te)/ Tackett, Philip, 13
Tacquet(te)/Tackett, Christopher, 12
Tacquet(te)/Tackett, Elizabeth, 13
Tacquet(te)/Tackett, Elizabeth/Betsy, 12
Tacquet(te)/Tackett, Francis, 12, 13
Tacquet(te)/Tackett, George, 12
Tacquet(te)/Tackett, James, 13
Tacquet(te)/Tackett, John, 12
Tacquet(te)/Tackett, Lewis, 13
Tacquet(te)/Tackett, Louis/Lewis, 12
TACQUET(TE)/TACKETT, Louis/Lewis, 12
Tacquet(te)/Tackett, Mary, 13
Tacquet(te)/Tackett, Peter, 12
Tacquet(te)/Tackett, Rachel, 12, 13
Tacquet(te)/Tackett, Sarah, 12

Tacquet(te)/Tackett, Thomas.
Tacquet(te)/Tackett, William, 13
Tacquet(te)/TackettLewis, 12
Tacquet(te)/Tsackett, William, 12
Tacquet, John, 12
Tacquet, Jr., Lewis, 12
Taylor, George, 17
Terrier, Anne, 32
Thompson, William, 17
Tietsoort, Jacob, 1
Toomer, Joshua, 14
TRABUE, Antoine, 34
Trabue, Magdeleine, 37
Trebue, Kath, 34
Tremble, Jeanne, 27
Turner, Elizabeth (Copley), 24
Turner, Praisever, 24
Tyler, John, 26
Tyler, John, President, 26

V

Valliant, Bennett, 35
Valliant, Dorothy, 36
Valliant, Elizabeth, 35
Valliant, James, 35
Valliant, Jean, 35
Valliant, John, 35
VALLIANT, John, 35
Valliant, Joseph, 35
Valliant, Mary, 35, 36
Valliant, Mary (X), 35
Valliant, Nicholas, 35
Valliant, Susanah, 36
Valliant, Thomas, 35
Valliant, William, 35
Van Der Stratten/Straeten, Magdelena, 11
Van Giesan, Crystyntje, 1
Van Horn, Jannetje, 1
Van Metre, Jan/John, 38
Van Siclen/Sichgelen, Ferdinandus, 1
Van Siclen/Sickelen/Sycklin, Eva, 1
Van Winkle, Antje, 1
VanderStraeten, Lodowycke, 11
Verreuil, Madeleine, 34
Verreuil, Madeleine (Prudon/Prudomme), 34
Verreuil, Moyse, 34
Videau, Elizabeth (Mauzé), 14
Videau, Jane, 14
Videau, Jeanne Elizabeth, 14
Videau, Jeanne Elizabeth Mauze, 14
Videau, Pierre, 14